IN CHRIST;

OR,

THE BELIEVER'S UNION WITH HIS LORD.

BY

A. J. GORDON,

PASTOR OF THE CLARENDON STREET CHURCH, BOSTON.

"Union with Christ is the distinctive blessing of the gospel dispensation in which every other is comprised, — justification, sanctification, adoption, and the future glorifying of our bodies ; all these are but different aspects of the one great truth, that the Christian is one with Christ."
EDWARD ARTHUR LITTON.

BOSTON:

GOULD AND LINCOLN,

59 WASHINGTON STREET.

1872.

PREFACE.

—◆—

IF this little book should be to any in
reading it, what it has been to the
author in writing it, an aid to meditation upon one of the deepest and tenderest
themes of the gospel, it will have served the
end of its publication.

It lays no claim to originality in doctrine,
having sought in every line to be in humble
subjection to the word of God, and constantly
to reflect whatever lesser light might fall
upon it from the thought and experience of
good men, since as has been fitly said, "*only*
'*with all saints*' can we comprehend what is
the depth and length of that which is presented to us in Jesus Christ."

If subjects have been touched upon which
are still in the list of disputed doctrine, they
have been brought forward, it is believed, in
the love of the truth as it is in Jesus, and not

in the interest of any sect or party ; while to controversy, " whose rough voice and unmeek aspect " have perhaps oftener repelled from the truth than won to it, no place has been given. With the humble prayer that its perusal may help some to rest in Christ with a deeper assurance, to abide in Him in greater spiritual fruitfulness, and to wait for his appearing with a more devout watchfulness, this book is now committed to the blessing of God and the use of his Spirit.

BOSTON, *April* 19, 1872.

CONTENTS.

		PAGE
I.	IN CHRIST. — INTRODUCTORY	7
II.	CRUCIFIXION IN CHRIST	27
III.	RESURRECTION IN CHRIST	47
IV.	BAPTISM INTO CHRIST	67
V.	LIFE IN CHRIST	89
VI.	STANDING IN CHRIST	113
VII.	PRAYER IN CHRIST	133
VIII.	COMMUNION IN CHRIST	151
IX.	SANCTIFICATION IN CHRIST	165
X.	GLORIFICATION IN CHRIST	183
	NOTES	201

I. INTRODUCTORY.

✠

Created in Christ Jesus unto good
works.   *Eph*. ii. 10.

Of Him are ye in Christ Jesus.
                          1 *Cor*. i. 30.

According as He hath chosen us in
Him before the foundation of the world.
                          Eph. i. 4.

And we are in Him that is true, even
in his Son Jesus Christ.
                          1 *John* v. 20.

✠

I.

IN CHRIST.

NO words of Scripture, if we except those, "God manifest in the flesh," hold within themselves a deeper mystery than this simple formula of the Christian life, " *in Christ*."

Indeed, God's taking upon Himself humanity, and yet remaining God, is hardly more inexplicable to human thought than man's becoming a " partaker of the divine nature," and yet remaining man. Both are of those secret things that belong wholly unto God. Yet, great as is the mystery of these words, they are the key to the whole system of doctrinal mysteries. Like the famous Rosetta stone, itself a partial hieroglyph, and thereby furnishing the long-sought clew to the Egyptian hieroglyphics, these words, by their very mystery, unlock all mysteries of the divine life, letting us into secrets that were " hidden

from ages and from generations." True, we
may not find in them an answer to the question, "*How* can these things be?" but we
shall see clearly that they *can* be. For
through this "Emmanuel knot of union," as
one has quaintly called it, those great facts of
the Christian life, regeneration, justification,
sanctification, and redemption, are drawn
up from the realm of the human and the
impossible, and made fast to Him with whom
"all things are possible." So that the question now becomes reversed, and we must ask,
"How can it be otherwise?" If one is in
Christ, he must have regeneration; for how
can the Head be alive, and the members dead?
If one is in Christ, he must be justified; for
how can God approve the Head, and condemn
the members? If one is in Christ, he must
have sanctification; for how can the spot-
lessly Holy remain in vital connection with
one that is unholy? If one is in Christ, he
must have redemption; for how can the Son
of God be in glory, while that which He has
made a part of his body lies abandoned in
the grave of eternal death?

And thus, through these two words, we get
a profound insight into the divine method of

salvation. God does not work upon the soul by itself; bringing to bear upon it, while yet in its alienation and isolation from Him, such discipline as shall gradually render it fit to be reunited to Him. He *begins* rather by re-uniting it to Himself, that through this union He may communicate to it that divine life and energy, without which all discipline were utterly futile. The method of grace is precisely the reverse of the method of legalism. The latter is holiness in order to union with God ; the former, union with God in order to holiness. Hence the Incarnation, as the starting-point and prime condition of recon-ciliation to God ; since there can be, to use Hooker's admirable statement, " no union of God with man, without that mean between both which is both." And hence the neces-sity of incorporation upon Christ, that what became *possible* through the Incarnation, may become *actual* and *experimental* in the indi-vidual soul through faith.

Nothing is more striking than the breadth of application which this principle of union with Christ has in the gospel. Christianity obliterates no natural relationships, destroys no human obligations, makes void no moral or spiritual laws. But it lifts all these up into a new sphere, and puts upon them this seal and signature of the gospel, *in Christ.* So that while all things continue as they were from the beginning, all, by their readjustment to this divine character and person, become virtually new. Life is still of God, but it has this new dependency " *in Christ.*" " Of Him are ye *in Christ Jesus.*" The obligation to labor remains unchanged, but a new motive and a new sanctity are given to it by its relation to Christ. " Forasmuch as ye know that your labor is not in vain *in the Lord.*" The marriage relation is stamped with this new signet, " Only *in the Lord.*" Filial obedience is exalted into direct connection with the Son of God. " Children obey your parents *in the Lord.*" Daily life becomes " a good conversation *in Christ.*" Joy and sorrow, triumph and suffering, are all *in Christ.* Even truth, as though needing a fresh baptism, is viewed henceforth " as it is *in Jesus.*" Death remains, but it is robbed of its sting and crowned with a beatitude, because in Christ. " Blessed are the dead who die *in the Lord.*"

Thus Christ, in taking man up into Himself, takes all that belongs to him. Instead

of rending him away from his natural con-
nections, He embraces all these with him
in Himself, that He may sanctify them all.
And not only is this true, but the opposite
and far more wondrous fact, namely, that
Christ, in raising man into union with Himself, raises him into all that belongs to *Him*,
into his divine life, and into partnership with
his divine work. So that he dies in his
death ; rises in his resurrection ; ascends in
his ascension ; is seated with Him in his
session at the Father's right hand ; and lives
in his eternal life.

So marked is this latter fact, that it has led
some to speak of the events of the Christian
life as affording " a striking parallel to those
of Christ's." But there is no parallel. Par-
allels never meet, while the very glory and
mystery of the believer's life is that it is one
with the Saviour's and inseparable from it.
It is not a life running alongside his, and
taking shape and direction from it. It is his
life reënacted in his followers ; the reproduc-
tion in them of those events which are im-
mortal in energy and limitless in application.

Our Lord's whole earthly career is one
continuous and living sacrament, of which his

disciples partake through faith.   And if their
eyes are not holden, they will discern, in each
great event of that life, not only the earnest
and symbol of what He works in them, but
they will see that only by feeding upon this
Bread, can they have any life dwelling in
them.   This — the blessed life and work of
our Lord — is his " body given for us ; " a
" body of divinity " containing all doctrine,
and nourishing with all life ; and of every
element of it — suffering, death, resurrection,
and glory — we hear Him saying, " Take, eat."

If we reflect upon the nature of that union
into which these words which we are considering link us, we see that every possible condition and requirement of salvation are met
and answered by it.

It is a union extending back of time.   We
find it clearly recognized in God's eternal
predestination.   " According as He hath chosen us *in Him* before the foundation of the
world."   " In *Him*."   It would seem as though
this were the focal point where alone the
beams of the Father's electing love met to
bless and comfort, while all beyond it was
darkness and death.   So vital is the atonement, that the shadow of the cross is thrown

back into a past eternity, to cover and justify God's choice of the sinner ;[1] and his very purpose of grace is wrapped up in Jesus Christ.[2]

If doubt suggests the query, " How could the believer be in Christ when he did not yet exist ? " the question can only be answered by another and deeper, " How could God elect and love a soul which He had not yet created ? " Yet that He did, is most explicitly declared in Scripture. And what David asserts of his natural body, not less emphatically does the Son of David assert of his mystical body. " Thine eyes did see my substance yet being imperfect, and in thy book *all my members were written,* which in continuance were fashioned, *when as yet there was none of them.*" Is there aught more painful than the searchings of the soul in the book of God's foreknowledge ? its irrepressible longings to know if it be written there ? If it goes alone in its solemn quest it will find no answer. But joining itself to Him who " was in the beginning with God," it hears Him saying, " Thou lovest *me* before the foundation of the world," and reverently appropriating the

[1] Rev. xiii. 8.   [2] 2 Tim. i. 9.

words in the secret right of faith, it joyfully
responds, "Herein is our love made perfect;
because *as He is so are we in this world.*"
The Father's eternal love for the Son, is the
pledge and certificate of his eternal love and
election of those who join themselves to that
Son.

But if this union runs back of time, it is
not less really in time a practical and present
reality; practical and present, because eternal.
For what is faith, but the suffrage of the soul
which ratifies and appropriates that election
of God which was made before creation?
Very literally is it

> "An affirmation and an act
> That bids eternal truth be present fact."

That which is given only in the divine intent
and foreordination, is not ours till we con-
sciously and believingly accept it. "Faith
cometh by hearing," and possession by faith.
God's choice of us lays hold of us only through
our choice of Him. And it is when the soul,
waking up to the fact of its sad alienation
from its Maker, and uttering its earnest "I
will arise and go unto my Father," joins itself
to that Father by a trusting faith, that the
Father, who in the Christ of eternity saw

him " *when he was yet a great way off,*" and
in the Christ of time crucified and slain *came
out to meet him,* becomes completely reconciled to him.

The first link of religion (*religo,* to bind
back) is the Incarnation, *God in Christ.* The
last is Faith, the *soul in Christ.* And when
the last has been joined to the first, the chain
is perfect. " I in them, and thou Father in
me, that they may be made perfect in one."

Again, the union of the believer with his
Lord is a *reciprocal* union. " Ye in me, and I
in you." Through it Christ both gives and
takes, — gives the Father's life and blessedness, and takes the believer's death and
wretchedness. " All that Christ has," says
Luther, " now becomes the property of the
believing soul ; all that the soul has, becomes
the property of Christ. Christ possesses
every blessing and eternal salvation ; they
are henceforth the property of the soul. The
soul possesses every vice and sin ; they become henceforth the property of Christ."

In this is most wonderfully displayed the
wisdom of the plan of redemption. Who that
has pondered the nature of sin, and thought
how radical, how ingrained, how thoroughly

2

a part of one's self it is, has not almost
doubted whether it could ever be taken away,
its evil principle exterminated, and the soul
completely disinfected of its taint? But when
we remember that Christ by his Cross deals
not only with sin, but with the nature in which
all its roots are imbedded, the way is plain ;
and we see with gratitude how the " body of
sin," that body which holds the germinant and
fertile principle of evil, may be destroyed,
and yet the sinner saved.

And who, on the other hand, that has contemplated the nature of that " holiness without which no man shall see the Lord," and
realized that it is no mere external morality,
no garment of righteousness to be assumed
and worn as the covering of a yet unsanctified nature ; but a divine life penetrating, pos-
sessing, and informing the soul, has not asked
despairingly, " How then can I, a sinner, hope
to be holy ? " But the gospel answer is all
in those three words, " I in you." He who
is the All-righteous, " is made unto us righteousness." So that to the soul that thirsts
after righteousness, it need no longer be said,
" The well is deep, and thou hast nothing
with which to draw." He is within it, " a

well of water springing up into everlasting
life."

Thus in Christ the twofold want of the
soul is met. It is emptied of self, and it is
filled with his fullness "who filleth all in all."

Can anything be so blessed for the believer
to realize, as this gracious interchange of life,
and character, and works, between himself
and his Lord? Oh, wondrous mystery! Christ
became the "Son of man," that we might become the "sons of God." He took upon
Himself our human nature, that we might be
made "partakers of the divine nature." He
was made sin for us, that we might be made
the "righteousness of God in Him."

And not less obviously do the terms of this
union suggest its *indissolubleness*. If joined
to the Lord by a mere external bond only, the
believer might well live in fear of being rent
from Him by the strain of fierce temptation.
But so transcendently intimate is this relation,
that the Holy Spirit even uses Christ and the
Church as interchangeable terms in the Scrip-
.tures. Now it is the human body that shadows forth the divine mystery. "As the body
is one and hath many members, and all the
members of that one body, being many, are

one body ; so also is Christ." [1] " Now ye are
the body of Christ and members in particular." And will Christ permit this body to be
dismembered ?   He can suffer in his members ; [2] but Faith would feel herself robbed of
all her heritage of assurance, were it any-
where written, He can be cut off or perish in
his members. Wounds and mutilations there
will be ; for, in Rutherford's strong phrase,
" The dragon will strike at Christ so long as
there is one bit or portion of his mystical
body out of heaven."   But love cannot cherish the fear that He will heal the hurts of his
people slightly, much less sunder them from
Him by an eternal excision.   For " No man
ever yet hated his own body, but *nourisheth*
and *cherisheth* it, even as the Lord the
Church ; for we are members of his body, of
his flesh, and of his bones." [3]

How clearly now this relation which we
bear to the Lord Jesus fixes two things, the
Christian experience and the Christian walk,
or the inner and outer life of the believer.

Christian experience is the making real in
ourselves, of what is already true for us in
Christ.[4]

[1] Note A.
[2] Acts xxii. 7.
[3] Eph. v. 29, 30.
[4] Note B.

" I am the vine, ye are the branches," says Christ. But the vine furnishes the branches not only with the principle of life, but with the type of life. No pressure or moulding from without is needed to shape them to the pattern of the parent stock. Every minutest peculiarity of form, and color, and taste, and fragrance, is determined by the root, and evolved from it. A true believer, therefore, will ask no better thing of the Lord, than "that the life also of Jesus may be made manifest in his body." For such a manifestation will, by a necessary law, be the unfolding within him of every needed element of joy and sorrow, of suffering and triumph.

It is not in any conventional standard of frames and feelings, that the disciple is to find the measure of attainment required of him. It is not by any painful reproducing of another's spiritual history that he is to acquire the true comfort of spirit which he longs for. Outward imitation, though it be of the Perfect Example himself, has little place in the order of spiritual growth ; little place because little possibility. " Without me," *i. e.,* apart from me, in separation from me, " ye can do nothing." To abide in Christ is the only secret of Christlikeness ; for only thus is attained the likeness of *unity*, which is perfect and enduring, instead of the likeness of *conformity*, which is only partial and transient.

How we misplace our experiences when we attempt, as mere copyists, to reproduce our Master's life within us. We put joy where the divine order would dictate sorrow, and nurse our sorrow, when the Lord would have us rejoice in Him. We reach after the unseasonable fruits of victory, when it is more needful as yet that we should endure the discipline of defeat, that so divine strength may be made perfect in our weakness. Our leaf withers in sere and yellow melancholy, when He would have it green and flourishing. What we would, that we continually do not, because we lack a true and steadfast hold on strength. Blessed is he, who, instead of seeking to attain the likeness of Christ as something only without him, realizes that he has been planted in that likeness. " He shall be like a tree planted by the rivers of water, that *bringeth forth his fruit in his season ; his leaf also shall not wither, and whatsoever he doeth shall prosper.*"

Never shall we attain a truly joyful Chris-

tian experience, therefore, till we learn that
holy living is neither the realization of some
ideal self, nor the imitation of some real saint.
" *For me to live is Christ.*" Christian progress is a growing *towards* Christ, by growing
from Him. And the Scripture exhortations
to high attainment in the divine life seem to
be based on this order. The believer is to
have "the mind of Christ" within him, the
" spirit of Christ" animating him. His development is a "growing up into Him in all
things who is the Head, even Christ." The
limit and boundary of his attainment is "the
perfect man," " the measure of the stature of
the fullness of Christ." Well may the disciple
set the Lord always before him as the ideal
of perfect attainment, if only he can have Him
thus always within him, as the source and
principle of daily growth.

We have said that our relation to Christ
determines also our Christian walk. This is
obvious.

A true Christian walk is a reproducing in
our lives of the righteousness which is already
ours in Christ.

Joined to the Lord by faith, we become
" partakers of his holiness." But not that

thereby we may be exempted from the necessity of personal holiness. It is rather that such personal holiness may have a new and higher obligation, since it has a new possibility. The double purpose of our union to Christ must never for a moment be forgotten, nor its heavenward and earthward aspects for an instant separated in our apprehension. It is in order that we may be as He is in the reckoning of God, and equally that we may be as He is before the eyes of men. "No condemnation to them that are in Christ Jesus," is one phase of this blessed truth. But, O believer, forget not the other, lest you bring upon yourself the curse of a dry and barren Antinomianism: "created in Christ Jesus *unto good works*, which God hath before ordained that we should walk in them."[1] The branches are the product and the measure of the roots, the one spreading as widely as the other strikes deeply. And how solemn the obligation resting upon those who are truly rooted in Christ, to reach forth their branches and cover that area of good works which they have underlaid, and, so to speak, preëmpted by their faith. Our

[1] Eph. ii. 10.

privileges in Jesus are glorious beyond comparison. But they are awful when we remember that they are the pledge and measure of our obligations. Never before on earth or perhaps in heaven was one exalted to utter so great a word as this, *I in Christ.* Yet if we know its meaning, we shall pause lest we speak it lightly or unadvisedly. "For he that saith he abideth in Him, ought himself also so to walk, even as He walked." [1]

Such are some of the germs of doctrine and life which are hidden for us in these words, and which it will be our purpose to unfold in the succeeding chapters.

If now we apprehend either the privileges or the duties into which this union brings us, we shall not be willing to regard it as a mere nominal thing, or to hold it as a cold doctrinal abstraction.

Nothing could be more real and more vital than this relationship.

We may speak of being regarded as in Him, and so having reckoned to us the benefits of his atonement. We may speak of being clothed with his righteousness, and so having his worthiness imputed to us. But

[1] 1 John ii. 6.

true as these expressions are, they do not reach the inwardness of meaning contained in the words, *in Christ,* or furnish an adequate statement of that deep interior fellowship into which God has called us in his Son.[1]

Truly that must be a most intimate bond which, beginning in Christ and encircling the disciple with its triple cords of faith, hope, and charity, ends again in Christ. "*From whom*" and "*into whom*," are the words that mark at once its origin and end, even that one Head who is the "Alpha and Omega, the Beginning and the End, the First and the Last."

"Here at length I beheld," says one, "the twofold mystery of love, that the Bride is both *of* Christ and *in* Christ. For as God took Eve from out the side of Adam, that she might be joined to him again in marriage, even so He frameth his Church out of the very flesh, the very wounded and bleeding side of the Son of man, that so in the sweet espousals of faith, he might 'present her as a chaste virgin to Christ.'[2] 'And they two shall be one flesh. This is a great mystery, but I speak concerning Christ and the Church.'"[3]

[1] 1 Cor. i. 8.   [2] 2 Cor. xi. 2.   [3] Eph. v. 32.

II. CRUCIFIXION IN CHRIST.

✠

I am crucified with Christ: nevertheless I live; yet not I, but Christ liveth in me. *Gal.* ii. 20.

Knowing this, that our old man is crucified with Him, that the body of sin might be destroyed, that henceforth we should not serve sin. *Rom.* vi. 6.

And they that are Christ's have crucified the flesh with the affections and lusts. *Gal.* v. 24.

✠

II.

CRUCIFIXION IN CHRIST.

"IT is one of the great principles of Christianity," says Pascal, "that everything which happened to Jesus Christ should come to pass in the soul and in the body of each Christian."

If by faith I am one with my Redeemer then, that term, "Christ crucified," involves another, "I, crucified with Christ." Hence we by no means reach the true measure of our inheritance in the Cross, when we regard the death of Christ as a formal transaction, by which One, eighteen hundred years ago, paid a debt that belonged to us, and thus secured our release from its obligation, we having no other connection with the event than that of recipients of its blessings. Paul saw a richer heritage for the saints than this. For with that key, *in Christ*, which opens for the believer all the wards of Christian doctrine and life, he lets us into "*the fellowship of his sufferings.*"

The great thought which filled his mind was his oneness with his Lord — a oneness not only of the present and the future, but equally of the past. And so he utters those grand but awful words, "*I have been crucified with Christ;*"[1] in which he carries himself back to the cross, and conceives of himself as so identified with the Redeemer, that he was with Him in his passion and obedience unto death, sharing, by a mysterious fellowship, not only the virtue but the endurance of the divine penalty.

And what was true for him is true for all who have come into that condition expressed by the words, "*in Christ Jesus.*"

That the crucifixion took place centuries ago, does not separate us from it at all. While as a historical event we assign it to a specific time and place, as a moral event it belongs to all time, and is just as near to us as it was to John or the Marys. "God manifested in the flesh," says Coleridge, "is eternity in the form of time." Christ crucified is an eternal fact realized at a certain date, but

[1] Note C.

touching all time with equal closeness. He
is "the Lamb slain from the foundation of the
world." In the eye of the *I am*, to whom all
time is an ever present now, this central fact
of the ages, the crucifixion, is an ever present
reality, and all souls that stand in moral relationship to it, stand so and have stood so
forever. Hence it can matter little to have
"known Christ after the flesh." Spiritual
union is entirely independent of all conditions of time and space. And in depth of
intimacy there can be no difference between
the believer of to-day and those who knew
our Lord on earth, since "by one Spirit we
are all baptized *into one body*," [1] and therefore
into one death, since "as many of us as were
baptized into Christ were baptized into his
death." [2]

How deeply, through the kindredship of the
flesh, *one* could share Christ's crucifixion, we
know. That the mother, watching beneath
the cross the agonies of her suffering Son,
endured in her own heart all the sharpness of
his death ; that as the soldiers thrust the spear
into his side, she knew in her own experience
the bitter meaning of the aged Simeon's

[1] 1 Cor. xii. 13.   [2] Rom. vi. 3.

prophecy, " Yea, a sword shall pierce through
thy own soul also," we can easily believe.
But since we have learned how nearer akin
Christ now is to all his brethren by the Spirit,
shall there seem to be anything less real in
the words of one who, by faith, clasped to his
heart the same cross of redemption, saying,
" I am crucified with Christ " ?

The mystery of that fellowship by which
we become sharers in Christ's death, we may
not presume to fathom. And yet it seems
clear how it must grow out of the terms of
the incarnation. Christ, in becoming man,
took our humanity into partnership in his
sacrificial work. Hence, his death is not
something merely made over to mankind as a
legacy of love ; it is something accruing to
it in this partnership of being.[1] But as
surely as He must be one with us by incarnation in order to *give* us part in his dying,
so surely must we be one with Him by faith,
that we may *take* part in his dying.

There is an inner and an outer circle of
redemption, if we may say so, both having a
common centre in the cross. The larger describes the limits of a possible and provisional
salvation ; the smaller those of an actual and

[1] Note D.

realized salvation. The whole world is com-
prehended in the one ; only those who believe are included in the other : "God who
is *the Saviour of all men, especially of those
who believe.*" [1] The relation which those in
the outer circle hold to Christ is that of members of the human race to its second Head.
The relation which those in the inner circle
hold to Him is that of members of the body
of Christ to the Head of the Church. The
first relation renders Christ's redemption
provisionally the redemption of every indi-
vidual of the race ; the second renders it actually such to every true believer. So that
when the Apostle says, "If one died for all,
then all died," [2] we understand his meaning to
be that all mankind died potentially in their
representative. Such is the blessed provision and stipulation, if we may say so, of the
atonement. But while He who could set no
limits to his love, " tasted death for every man,"
alas ! how many refuse to taste his death, and
through faith owning themselves one with
Him, to taste their own death to sin in his !

As clearly now as we are forbidden by the
Scriptures to extend the possibility of a vital

[1] 1 Tim. iv. 10. [2] 2 Cor. v. 14.*

3

and saving union to Christ beyond the boundaries of this inner circle of redemption, so clearly should our faith in the reality of the Christian's oneness with his Lord forbid us to admit such words as " nominal " and " judicial " *within* the limits of this inner circle. Here we are beyond all legal fictions. " We are *in Him that is true.*" And as fully as we believe that his death was real, and no vain proffer, so must we believe that our death in Him was real, since we are members of his body. The cross deals not with our sins apart from ourselves. It permits us not to lay our transgressions upon the Divine victim, and yet stand ourselves afar off, and without personal communion with his sufferings. In the typical sacrifice, the hands of the offerer were laid upon the head of the offering, and thus was declared the identity of the offerer and the offering. In the antitype, faith lays its hand upon the head of the Lamb of God, not simply that it may thereby transfer guilt to the guilt-bearer, but that it may join in solemn unity of suffering, the sinner and the sin-offering. Thus the judgment of the cross is intensely personal. Not sin only, but nature ; not nature only, but personality is there brought to trial. "Knowing this, that *our old man* was crucified with Him."[1] The nail that pierced the handwriting of ordinances that was against us to blot it out, went deeper, and transfixed also the subjects of those ordinances to inflict on them the penalty it prescribed. And now henceforth we behold Christ and his Church scarred with the same wounds. And they who once could only ask of the Redeemer, "What are these wounds in *thy* hands?" can now answer their question by showing their own hands and saying, "I bear in my body the marks of the Lord Jesus."

While now some reject this heritage of the cross by their denial of Christ, many also by denying Adam's sin deny Christ's death, and thrust it from them! The bitterest repining which the human heart has ever known has been against that utterance of the Spirit, "By one man's disobedience many were made sinners."[2] But may it not be that that solemn law which makes the fall of one involve the fall of many, is the only law which could make the rising of one to be the rising of many? A common nature ruined

---

[1] Rom. vi. 6.*   [2] Rom. v. 19.

would seem even by its overshadowing curse
to proclaim the possibility of a common nature redeemed. Who knows whether, if men
could only have sinned and fallen as separate
units, they must not have been restored by separate redemptions? We will not speculate
on such a theme. Rather will we joyfully return to what God has revealed, that as in the
sin of one " all sinned," [1] so in the penal death
of one " all died." [2] *All died!* Wonderful
words! Christ's death does not supersede
ours. It implies and recognizes it, as, in the
civil compact, the vote of the representative
implies the vote of the people. What Christ
did *for* us, was done *by* us in the divine reckoning, because done by Him who was *of* us
as Head and Surety. [3] We say Christ died
that we might live. In a deeper sense it is
true that He died that we might *die;* might
die a death painless to ourselves but satisfying to the law — a death of such intensity
and merit that it should expiate at once the
penalty of our sins, instead of requiring an
eternity of woe. O, blessed privilege! " *Ye
shall indeed drink of my cup,*" is a promise
realized unto us as well as unto the two disci-

[1] Rom. v. 12.   [2] 2 Cor. v. 14.   [3] Note E.

ples. But it is only a cup of blessing to us.
He drank the vinegar and gall of pain and
agony. He leaves us only the precious wine
of consolation. And thus we enter into communion with his sufferings, and become partakers of his death. " If one died for all, then
all died." But how differently the One from
the all ! He bore the pain of death ; they
bear only the merit of it. He gives infinite
worthiness to the act by his divinity ; they
receive the purchase of the act in their humanity. And yet nothing is deducted from
the full assurance that they have died. Such
" is the personal initiation into the mystery
of sacrifice" which we receive through faith.

We see at once where this blessed fact
places us — even in perfect reconciliation to
a violated law. God has said, " The soul that
sinneth, it shall die." The soul has sinned,
and it has died in Christ. The law has said,
" Cursed is every one that continueth not in
all things which are written in the book of
the law to do them." None have continued
in obedience. But Christ hath been " made
a curse for us ; " for it is written, *"Cursed is
every one that hangeth on a tree."* Hence,
crucified with Christ, we have been accursed

in Him. Not one jot or tittle has then passed away from the law, but all has been fulfilled.[1]

How affecting this perfect literalness, this rigid honesty, if we may call it so, in the dealings of our Surety with the law! And with what triumphant assurance it enables us to take up and repeat that verdict of our acquittal from condemnation, "*He that hath died hath been justified from sin.*"[2]

But, alas! how slow is our faith to enter into the fullness of this gospel! As that deep hunger for expiation which the sense of sin begets, begins to gnaw the soul, many seek to appease it by mere self-crucifixion. If not with the scourge and sackcloth of the ascetic, yet with the vinegar and gall of sharp remorse; with the compunctions of a bleeding and unhealed heart, striving to satisfy that law, which, from the soul of man as well as from the statute-book of God, proclaims that without the shedding of blood there is no remission. Nothing is more painful to behold than this search for the cross, which ends only in a wounded self; in a conscience that is laying on itself the chastisement of its

[1] Note F.   [2] Rom. vi. 7.*

peace, and in a broken spirit that is striving to heal itself with its own stripes. The gospel neither demands nor will take any such offering from the sinner. Reversing that well-known sentiment of legalism, its emphatic declaration is, —

> " The cross in thine own heart will never save thy soul,
> The cross on Golgotha alone can make thee whole."

Here, as everywhere, the Master's words meet us, to call us away from all self-help. "Without me ye can do nothing." As high as the heaven is above the earth, so far is the distance from the self-crucifixion to *crucifixion in Christ.*[1] To pass from the one to the other requires but a single trusting look of faith. But it is to cross " the whole diameter of being" between the spotless Lamb of God and the guilty children of men. That there is a sacrificing of self that is in-

---

[1] How vivid a reflection of his own experience do we find in Luther's pithy comment on these words : " I am crucified with Christ." " Paul speaketh not here of crucifying by imitation or example ; but he speaketh of that *high crucifying* whereby sin, the devil, and death, are crucified in Christ and not in me. Here Christ Jesus doth all Himself alone. But believing in Christ, I am by faith crucified also with Christ ; so that all these things are crucified and dead with me." — *Commentary on Galatians.*

separable from the gospel idea of discipleship
is unquestionable. But it is not that which
is wrought for obtaining peace with God, but
that which grows out of a peace already ob-
tained in the crucified Christ. The whole
course of the divine life is from Christ to self,
and not from self to Christ. To begin an expiation in one's own sufferings, hoping that it
may end in fellowship and union with Christ's
sufferings, is not only to transpose, but completely to vitiate the order of grace. There
is nothing of ours, soul, body, or spirit, that is
without blemish. And when we understand
that our very tears need themselves to be
washed in the blood of the Redeemer, and
our very penitence to be sanctified in his exceeding sorrow, we shall gladly turn wholly
to the perfect offering. And so from that re-
liance on penance and mortification, which,
however sincere, is an obtrusion of self into
that realm of sacrifice which Christ alone can
fill ; and from that searching in a bruised and
excruciated conscience for peace, which, however honest, is but an attempt to discover in
self that sin-offering which can only be found
in the bleeding Lamb of God, how gratefully
we turn to Christ crucified as our only true

resting place for comfort! " Let me know that I have repented enough and suffered enough," is the voice of a faith that is still in bondage to law. The voice of a faith that is free is, " Let me hear that Christ died in the stead of sinners, of whom I am chief; that He was forsaken of God, during these fearful agonies, because He had taken my place; *that on his cross I paid the penalty of my guilt* Let me hear too that his blood cleanseth from all sin, and that I may now appear before the bar of God, not only pardoned, but innocent. Let me realize the great mystery of the recip- rocal substitution of Christ and the believer, or rather their perfect unity, He in them and they in Him, which He has expressly taught; and let me believe that *I was in effect cruci- fied on Calvary*, and He will in effect stand before the throne in my person ; his the pen- alty, mine the sin ; his the shame, mine the glory ; his the thorns, mine the crown ; his the merit, mine the reward. Verily, thou shalt answer for me, O Lord, my Redeemer. In Thee do I put my trust, let me never be confounded." [1]

Do we ask then what our death in Christ

[1] Bishop Le Jeune.

has accomplished for us ? What has it not accomplished ? Like the flaming sword which drove man out of Paradise, and which *turned every way*, to keep the tree of life, this weapon of redemption with which the Captain of our salvation opened the kingdom of heaven to all believers, presents a destroying edge to every foe that stands across our track.

The *world*, whose friendship has been our deepest enmity to God, because drawing our best affections and diverting our truest life from Him, is at last overcome. The cross has sundered us from its enslaving bondage. "*By whom the world is crucified unto me, and I unto the world.*" Allure us for a season it may ; draw us to its pleasures it sometimes will. But from the moment we know ourselves dead with Christ, its tyranny is broken. "*How shall we who died to sin, live any longer therein ?*"[1] To go back to the world from which we have thus been separated, we must despise the cross of our redemption, trampling on the blood of the covenant wherewith we are sanctified, and compelling our Master to retrace the *Via Dolorosa* of his agony, that we may crucify Him afresh, and put Him to an open shame.

[1] Rom. vi. 2.*

The *flesh*, warring against the Spirit, violat-
ing every truce with conscience, breaking
every covenant which we have made with
God — behold, this enemy from whom we
cannot flee, has yet received his death wound.
Christ put a nail through him when He gave
his own body to the smiters. " And they that
are Christ's have crucified the flesh with the
affections and lusts." Wounded unto death,
yet struggling for his lost dominion, we shall
never be wholly quit of him, till the grave
closes over him. But in God's reckoning we
are even now delivered. " Ye are not in the
flesh but in the Spirit." Upon our natural
and guilt-attainted man, justice has executed
his death-warrant, and is satisfied. In words
traced by the infallible spirit of truth, we have
the record of his decease: "*Ye died*, and
your life is hid with Christ in God." [1]

When the Judge calls for us now as He did
of old for Adam, saying, "*Where art thou?*"
He will no longer seek the living among the
dead. Our life, the life of which He now
takes cognizance, *is hid in Christ*. In Him
will He find it, and not in the charnel-house
of our dead man. What are these evil habits

[1] Col. iii. 3.*

that are still clinging about us, but the relics
of that old and crucified nature ! What are
these sins that pain us and make us cry out
with sorrow, but the motions and death throes
of that body that has been doomed by the decree of the cross ! Confess them sorrowfully
and with shame we must ; but we may tri-
umphantly own that "they belong to the old
man, and we are carrying them to the grave
to be buried with their owner." Even Satan,
the head and instigator of all other enemies,
has been disarmed and doomed. Christ took
on flesh that He might destroy him that had
the power of death, that is, the devil, and
"deliver them who, through fear of death,
were all their life-time subject to bondage."

Rejoice, then, O saint, in your rescue from
"the Terrible Captain and his standard-
bearer." On Calvary, Christ triumphed over
death by becoming the victim of death. That
eternal terror that was once before you, He by
his cross has put forever behind you. It cannot cast one threatening shadow across your
pathway now. It cannot wring one pang of
foreboding agony from your soul. "Death
stung itself to death, when it stung Christ."[1]

[1] Romaine.

Recognizing now the realness of this union with Christ in his death, and the fullness of blessing that grows therefrom, it only remains for the believer to make the truth real to his own experience. Beholding how God has set Christ's death to our account, through our partnership with Him, set it also yourself to your account and take possession of the riches of grace and mercy which are thus made yours. " In that He died, He died unto sin once. . . . Likewise *reckon ye also yourselves to be dead indeed unto sin.*"

We will by no means say that this reckoning will be painless. Adam's nature dies hard within us ; and before we can own the justice of its sentence, or acquiesce in its condemnation, there will doubtless be wrought within us, by the Holy Spirit, some bitter experimental fellowship with Christ's sufferings. Our sins will find us out, and the death that is by sin. We shall feel the terrible dealing of our Judge with our consciences. There will be strong crying and tears ; perhaps the darkness of desertion, the rending of the rocky heart, and the sense of deserved wrath piercing the soul as with a two-edged sword. It may be long before we can yield up the

ghost of the natural man and renounce al
trust in him forever. But once enabled to account ourselves dead in Him, what a deliverance is ours!

Standing by the cross now, we discern in
the gloom and power of darkness that gather
round it, that "outer darkness" which had
been ours forever out of Christ. In that
plaintive "*Eloi, Eloi,*" we hear what had been
our cry of despair unanswered forever, except
we had been found in Him. In that dread-
ful rending cry which delivers up the spirit,
we own the due reward of our deeds, while
confessing that this man hath done nothing
amiss. But now all these things are passed
forever both for Him and for us, as soon as
the "*It is finished*" has been spoken. And
lo! the foregleams of the resurrection break
upon us. The light of a certain and triumphant hope enters our heart. Remembering
that we are joined to Him who said, "I lay
down my life that I may take it again," we
cease from tears and follow Him, saying as
we hasten onward, " Now if we be dead with
Him, we believe that we shall also live with
Him."

III. RESURRECTION IN CHRIST.

✠

If ye then be risen with Christ, seek those things which are above, where Christ sitteth on the right hand of God.

Col. iii. 1.

God, who is rich in mercy, for his great love wherewith He loved us, even when we were dead in sins, hath quickened us together with Christ; (by grace ye are saved;) and hath raised us up together, and made us sit together in heavenly places, in Christ Jesus.

Eph. ii. 4–6.

And you, being dead in your sins and the uncircumcision of your flesh, hath He quickened together with Him, having forgiven you all trespasses.

Col. ii. 13.

✠

III.

RESURRECTION IN CHRIST.

ONE with Christ in his dying, we must be one with Him also in his resurrection. For the bands of this mystic union are not dissolved or weakened while the Saviour lies in the tomb. Joined to his people, that He might carry them with Him through the pains and penalties of death, He now in the same gracious partnership of being brings them up again from the dead. And so "He spreads the mighty miracle of his own regeneration from the dead, along the whole line of history. He repeats it in every true believer. The Church's is an everlasting Easter."[1]

There is doubtless the same theoretical difficulty in conceiving of the believer as having been raised in Christ's resurrection, as there is in conceiving of Him as having died

[1] Archer Butler.

in his crucifixion. And hence, as some read
that very striking and explicit word of the
Spirit, "If then ye were raised together with
Christ,"[1] they find it much easier to remand
the expression to the realm of metaphor, than
to accept it literally and without condition.

But we are to remember that the resurrection is not merely a historical fact, the trans-
cendent miracle and mystery of the apostolic age. Certainly it is all that. But it is
more. It is a moral event, a principle of
spiritual energy, as well as a fact of human
history. While to those therefore who see
Christ only from the outer court of knowledge, and whose faith ends in the bare belief
that "He died and rose again *according to
the Scriptures*," the mystery may remain:
to those who press into the inner sanctuary
of fellowship, praying that they may "know
Him and the *power of his resurrection*," it
will be more and more laid open to them as
they advance. What the power of Christ's
resurrection is, we may infer from the closeness of its relation in the gospel to spiritual
renewal and justification, as well as to physical reanimation.

[1] Col. iii. 1.*

It is a judicial power, and it is a regenera-
tive power. The first only as crowning and
sealing the judgment of the cross, so that
whereas Christ's death was our justification
procured, his rising was our justification justified. And the second only as related to the
Spirit, so that while it is the Holy Ghost that
renews, it is clearly only from the risen
Christ that the soul derives its life in renewal.
"Because I live, ye shall live also."

Let us trace these two thoughts into their
details. How clearly our resurrection is
linked with Christ's, for the assurance of pardon, in this passage : "And you, being dead
in your sins and the uncircumcision of your
flesh, *hath He quickened together with Him,
having forgiven you all trespasses."* [1] That
forgiveness was fully accomplished when He
had pronounced the "It is finished" on the
cross. For then had He blotted out the
dark score of disobedience that was against
us, having nailed it to the cross. And this
verily was decisive and final, "a nail fastened
in a sure place." But the pardon thus written in his blood waited to be sealed and at-
tested by his resurrection. For though He

[1] Col. ii. 13.

had spoiled principalities and powers by his
death, only by bursting the bars of the grave
could He "make a show of them, openly tri-
umphing over them in Himself."

And so, while in the blood of the dying
Christ we see the title of our pardon, we wait
for a luminous glance from the risen Christ
to bring it out into full distinctness and significance. An inheritance may be ours and
yet not ours ; ours in effect, because the deed
of it has been executed ; but not ours to
certain knowledge and apprehension, since
we have not received it. The heritage of
peace which became ours by the death of the
Testator, faith cannot take while He lies in
the grave. We must see our Eliakim, who
openeth and no man shutteth, returning from
the tomb with the key of the House of David
laid upon his shoulder,[1] before we can enter
with Him into our purchased possession.
So vital is this to our assurance of faith, that
Paul says, " If Christ be not raised, your
faith is vain, *ye are yet in your sins.*"[2] Ye
died with Christ, ye in Him and He in your
sins that were upon Him ; ye were buried
with Christ, ye in Him still, and He in your

------

[1] Isaiah xxii. 22.   [2] 1 Cor. xv. 17.

sins still. If He lies yet in that dark un-
opened grave, ye lie there yet, in your sins,
because in Him who went down into the tomb
with those sins upon Him. Faith cannot
place the disciple above his Master. It can
only make him to be as his Master, a sharer
in his condition, a partner in his destiny.
Now while our Lord's sufferings in the flesh
were completed when He yielded up the
ghost, He was not disentangled from our
guilt so long as He lay in the tomb. How
then shall our faith outrun Him, and reach
the vantage ground of the resurrection, while
the grave still holds Him in its grim impris-
onment? How shall we break the bands of
condemnation and cast away its cords from
us, if it be possible for Him to be " holden of
death?" And yet He is so holden, if a single item of the debt of sin is left uncanceled.
" The wages of sin is death ; " and that wages
must be paid to the full. " Thou shalt by no
means come out thence till thou hast paid
the uttermost farthing," says an inexorable
law ; and if He is holden, we are holden with
Him, because of that faith that has linked us
into indissoluble partnership with his destiny.
Such is the certain inference from that dreary
hypothesis, " If Christ be not raised."

" But now *is* Christ risen from the dead."
And since we are risen with Him, we are not
in our sins. In his renewal from the dead,
we were lifted forever from their dark enfold-
ing condemnation. They cannot bind a single fetter on us now ; they cannot remand us
for a single instant to the prison-house of
despair. Because " the God of peace has
brought again from the dead our Lord Jesus
Christ, that great Shepherd of the sheep," all
the flock folded in Him by faith, are safe.
" They shall never perish, neither shall any
man pluck them out of his hands."

That the remains of sin are still clinging
to us, we are only too painfully conscious.
Not like the sinless Lord have we put off all
the cerements of our body of death. Walking with Him in the same resurrection, we
are as yet like Lazarus bound hand and foot
with the grave-clothes — the habits of sin
that still cling to us, the power of evil that
enthralls us ; and we wait in eager expect-
ancy the last resurrection word that shall
say, " Loose him, and let him go." But not
the less truly are we alive with Christ from
the dead, and death, the penalty of sin, can
have no more dominion over us.

This truth is most strikingly told again in those words of the Apostle, " Who was delivered for our offenses, and raised again for our justification," — literally, " delivered *because* of our offenses, and raised *because* of our justification." [1] So enwrapped was He in our sins that were upon Him, that he could not escape from death. But when the justification of us who are in Him had been accomplished, He could not be detained by death. And so because our justification was completed, He was raised again. What an affecting emphasis is here again laid upon the doctrine of our Lord's union with his people ! Their cause is so thoroughly his own that He cannot outstrip them a single step in the path of redemption. Opener of the prison doors to them that are bound, He yet waits till the last demand of justice has been satisfied, before He comes through the gate of the grave to lead them out. The members must be with their Head. They are his fullness, and without them He cannot be made perfect. He waits till the weary hours of their prison service are completed in their Surety. He cannot accept deliverance while they are un-

[1] Note G.

der condemnation. But when the full acquittal has been secured, the glorious promise is fulfilled, " *The third day I shall be perfected.*" Aye, thou mighty Captain of our
Salvation, thou first Begotten from the dead,
because thou wilt then have "*perfected forever them that are sanctified.*"

I am aware of a certain holy jealousy for
the honor of the cross, that restrains some
from ascribing justifying efficacy to the resurrection of Christ. But let it be marked ·
that it is not atoning justification which we
attribute to it, but "*manifestive justification,*" as Edwards so exactly names it. And
a guilty conscience needs this as well as the
other. The prisoner does not know himself
free, though he has served out to its last day
and hour his term of sentence, if the prison
doors still remain shut upon him. Prisoners
of hope, bound with Christ under the law, we
are not fully assured of our deliverance, when
we can reckon ourselves dead with Him,
though justice is thereby satisfied. We wait
for the angel to descend from heaven — mes-
senger of peace to us because deputy of justice to Him — to roll back the stone from the
door of the sepulchre. The wounded hands

and feet, the dying cry that yields up the
Spirit, and the lifeless body at last lying in
the tomb, are the tokens of the price paid.
But the empty tomb, the folded napkin, and
the linen clothes laid by themselves, these
are the tokens of the price accepted, of the
prisoner's discharge, and of the loosing of the
pains of death forever, from all who died in
Christ. And so to all questionings of a timid
or doubting conscience, the answer now is,
"Who is he that condemneth? It is Christ
that died, *yea rather, that is risen again,* who
is even at the right hand of God, who also
maketh intercession for us." [1]

But not only does our resurrection in
Christ raise us out of condemnation ; it also
lifts us into a new life in Him. In Christ
crucified we put off the old man, in Christ
risen we put on the new man. The cross
was for the destruction of the body of sin ;
the resurrection was for imparting to us the

[1] Rom. viii. 34.
"Le Chrétien éclairé sur la résurrection de notre Sau-
veur jouit de l'assurance de son salut ; il en est aussi sûr,
qu'il est sûr que Jésus Christ est ressuscité ; et pour le
faire douter de son espérance éternelle, il faudrait com-
mencer par le faire douter que Jésus Christ est ressuscité
des morts." — *Adolphe Monod.*

principle of divine life. By his crucifixion,
our Redeemer accomplished a twofold death
for us. *He condemned sin in the flesh,*[1] ex-
hausting at once the eternal penalties that
were menacing the soul of man, and inflicting
on the body that death sentence which will
be fully consummated for every believer when
he lies down in the grave. By his resurrection He makes us the subjects of a twofold
regeneration — the regeneration of the soul
in this life, and that of the body in the life to
come ; both of which are expressly said to
make us sons of God, because the one only
completes and consummates the other ; and
in both of which we are " the children of God,
being children of the resurrection."

For the renewed body we still wait with
all saints in eager longing till we be clothed
upon at the resurrection. The renewed soul
we already have in Christ. " Blessed be the
God and Father of our Lord Jesus Christ,
which according to his abundant mercy, *hath
begotten us again* unto a lively hope, by the
resurrection of Jesus Christ from the dead."[2]
Wonderful words ! It is not merely a poten-
tial renewal that is here indicated, the laying

[1] Rom. viii. 3.   [2] 1 Pet i. 3.

of a basis for a possible but still future regeneration. We that believe, are already "risen
with Him, through the faith of the operation
of God." The old life, with its kindredship to
Adam, with its heritage of his curse, with its
clinging incubus of his death, is put off at his
grave. In the second Adam we now live.
And "as He is, so are we in this world." He
is "the first fruits of them that slept."[1] "And
if the first fruits be holy, so also is the lump."
He is "declared to be the Son of God with
power by the resurrection from the dead."
In the same divine recognition do we likewise
receive the adoption of sons. Willingly as He
endured the cross, despising the shame, did
He say, "*My* God, *my* God, why hast Thou
forsaken me," making no mention of us for
whom He was forsaken. But now, as He is
about to sit down at the right hand of the
throne of God, bringing all the members of
his mystical body to be seated with Him in
the heavenly places, we hear Him saying, " I
ascend unto *my* Father and *your* Father, unto
my God and *your* God," thus suggesting with
the most exquisite tenderness their oneness
with Him in his now recovered fellowship.

[1] 1 Cor. xv. 20.

What a place then does the sepulchre of
Jesus occupy! It is the border line and
meeting place of law and grace. It is the
solemn pause, "the divine ellipsis" in the
work of redemption, whence we look back
upon the old nature, the old sin, and the old
curse, and forward upon the "all things" that
"are become new." Standing here and looking either way, we see how Christ's work
divides itself into what he did as the Sin-
bearer, and what he did as the Life-giver.

In his *Crucifixion*,	In his *Resurrection*,
He was —	He was —
"Delivered for our of-fenses."	"Raised again for our jus-tification." (Rom. iv. 25.)
"Put to death in the flesh."	"Quickened in the Spirit." (1 Pet. iii. 18.)
"In that He died, He died unto sin, once."	"In that He liveth, He liveth unto God." (Rom. vi. 10.)
"He was crucified through weakness."	"Yet He liveth by the power of God." (2 Cor. xiii. 4.)

By his death, He became the "end of the
law to every one that believeth;" by his resurrection, He became "the beginning, the first-
born from the dead." *There* the root of the
first Adam was wounded unto death. *Here*

humanity springs up anew, and from a new
and incorruptible seed. "*I am the true Vine,*"
says Christ. All the culture and pruning of
Judaism had failed to bring the stock of the
first Adam to any satisfying fruitfulness. "I
had planted thee a noble vine," says Jehovah,
"wholly a right seed; how art thou turned
into the degenerate plant of a strange vine
unto me."[1] Christ risen from the dead was
given to be a *new stock*, the elect and best of
all the vineyard of heaven. The crucifixion
was the uprooting of the old, the crushing of
its very roots as well as the clusters of its
grapes in the wine-press of the wrath of God.
The resurrection was the upspringing of the
new, the true vine. And all who are truly
renewed, are shoots and branches of that. To
be incorporated upon that vine, — to abide in
it, — this is the only way of life, because the
only way to become a partaker of the divine
nature. And yet how many are trying to-day
to revive the *old*, digging about that scathed
and unfruitful stump of Adam's nature, hoping
to restore it.—The sacramentarian, sprinkling
it with the "baptismal dew," thinking that
"through the scent of water it may bud and

[1] Jer. ii. 21.

bring forth boughs like a plant ; " not remembering that by the death and burial of our
Lord, the " root thereof has waxed old in the
earth, and *the stock thereof has died in the
ground.*" — The moralist, lopping off dead
branches and pruning away excrescences,
hoping to make it nobly productive ; not remembering that by the crucifixion of Christ,
" the axe has been laid at the root of the
tree."

To be in Christ the risen man, then, is to
have eternal life. We no longer trace our
genealogy back to Adam now. That registry
has been annulled for those whose names are
written in the Lamb's Book of Life. The
night that covered Joseph's tomb was the last
of the old dispensation. The resurrection
light that broke at length upon that tomb
was the day-dawn of the new. Only from
that day does the Church of the redeemed
begin. " Date it rather from the day of Pentecost," does some one say ? But Resurrection, Ascension, and Pentecost would seem to
be only successive stages of the same great
transaction, the bringing of the Church into
the fullness of the divine life. For Christ's
ascent bodily marks his descent spiritually ;

his taking our nature up unto God the bringing down of God's life to us, and the com-
mencement of his dwelling in us by his Spirit.

And this is our risen life, however we conceive or speak of it, that we are in Him and
He in us. It is a life as far removed from
that of Adam as the heaven from the earth,
the constant partaking of Christ who is the
Life. And this is our righteousness, not the
name or the credit of holiness merely, but the
righteousness of God perpetually upon us,
because of our identification with Him who
is made unto us righteousness.

The Resurrection of our Lord then is not
merely a pledge of our own ; it is our own if
we are his.[1] All that it did for Him, we may
boldly say it did for us if we are in Him.
True, in experience much of its blessing is
yet future and embryonic to us, as it is not to

[1] And our unbelief is naught else than a guilty forfeiture
of what has been graciously bequeathed to us by Christ, a
refusal to be embraced in that resurrection which has already in the intention and provision of God embraced us.
George Herbert touches this thought very delicately in those
lines, —

    " Arise sad heart ; *if thou dost not withstand,*
    Christ's resurrection thine may be ;
    Do not by hanging down break from the hand,
    Which, as it riseth, raiseth thee."

Him. But because of our perfect identity
with Him, with Him to whom the possible and
the actual are ever the same, all is counted
as present to us. With Him we are " not in
the flesh, but in the Spirit." With Him we
are "seated in the heavenly places." Hence
that same strenuous demand which the Scriptures lay upon us for realizing our death in
Christ: "Reckon ye yourselves to be dead indeed," they lay upon us for realizing our resurrection in Him : " Seek those things which
are above, where Christ sitteth on the right
hand of God."

And can we conceive of any more effective
motive to Christian attainment, than this?
In Christ Jesus we work no longer *for* life,
but *from* life. Our high endeavor is not to
shape our actual life in the flesh into conformity to an ideal life that is set before us
in Him. It is rather to reduce our true life
now hid in Christ, to an actual life in our-
self. And so the summons of the gospel is,
not that we behold what is possible for us in
Christ, and reach forth to it ; but rather that
we behold what is accomplished for us in
Christ, and appropriate it and live in it.
Risen with Christ, the first-fruits of· our

spirits already carried up with Him into
glory, our life hid with Him in God, how
shall not our heart be where our treasure is?
How shall not our love be ever kindling
and burning upwards, purging itself of all
earthly dross, till it is wholly intent on Him?
Why hang the damps and corruptions of the
grave about us still, earthliness and sinful
affections, and all these clinging accompani-
ments of moral death, from which our Lord has
ransomed us? It is ours even now to walk
with Him in white, and to be ever "breath-
ing with Him the freshness of the morning of the resurrection and of endless life."
Risen with Him, how shall we not more and
more recognize our life as in heaven, and be
waiting for Him who is our life to appear?
Not as the sorrowing Man of Nazareth, not
as the sinless sufferer of Calvary, do we wait
to see Him now. " *The root and the offspring
of David,*" for awhile " cut off, though not for
Himself," He comes again to sit upon the
throne of his father David. " *The bright and
morning star,*" hidden now behind that cloud
that has for a little time received Him out of
our sight, He soon shall startle the world by
the "brightness of his coming." And be-

5

cause we are seated with Him now in the
heavenly places, we shall be seated with Him
in the earthly ; because our life is one with
his now, his manifestation shall be our manifestation. " When Christ, who is our life, shall
appear, then shall ye also appear with Him in
glory."

And so we wait patiently till the " day
dawn, and the day-star arise in our hearts."

IV. BAPTISM INTO CHRIST.

✠

For as many of you as have been bap=
tized into Christ, have put on Christ.
Gal. iii. 27.

Know ye not that so many of us as
were baptized into Christ, were bap=
tized into his death? Therefore we are
buried with Him by baptism into death,
that like as Christ was raised up from
the dead by the glory of the Father, even
so we also should walk in newness of
life. *Rom.* vi. 3–4.

Buried with Him in baptism, where=
in also ye are risen with Him, through
the faith of the operation of God, who
hath raised Him from the dead.
Col. ii. 12.

✠

IV.

BAPTISM INTO CHRIST.

EAD with Christ, and risen with Christ! How perfectly has the Spirit enshrined this twofold doctrine for us in the initial ordinance of the gospel! Baptism is at once the rite in which the believer gives token of his union with Jesus in his death and resurrection, and in which he receives in germ all those deep kindred truths which are to unfold with his daily growth in faith and knowledge; the sacrament which the Church holds as a perpetual trust from her ascended Lord, and which holds for the Church in perpetual preservation this doc- trine in which her life is bound up.

If we have assented then to what has been said in the foregoing chapters, and if we have "obeyed from the heart that *form* [1] of doc- trine" to which we are thus committed, we

[1] Note II.

shall have now no hesitating answer for the
question of the Apostle, " Know ye not that
so many of us as were baptized into Jesus
Christ, *were baptized into his death ?* " Nor
having assented to this shall we be uncertain
as to his conclusion, " *Therefore we were buried*[1] *with Him by baptism into death, that like
as Christ was raised up from the dead by the
glory of the Father, even so we also should
walk in newness of life."* [2]

And so we look back to that solemn moment when, in the name of the Trinity, we
were immersed beneath the water, and then
raised again from the parted wave, and we see
in the act the divine credential which our
Lord gave to our consenting faith of our
union with Him in his dying and rising ; or in
the expressive phrase of Chrysostom, " the
sign and pledge of our descent with Him
into the state of the dead, and of our return
thence."

How far we must ever keep from ascribing
any saving efficacy to the water, or to the
ritual act of baptism, will appear when we
consider how wonderfully framed the ordinance is for disclaiming all merit for the be-

[1] Note I.   [2] Rom. vi. 3, 4.

liever's obedience, in the very act of helping
him to render that obedience. For not only
is here a sign which is empty and worthless,
without the accompanying faith, but one
which shows how empty that faith is without
its object, Christ crucified and risen. Re-
pentance, belief, obedience, what are these
apart from the Redeemer, and except as
methods of appropriating his redemption?
God reads them, and will have us express
them in the terms of the Saviour's atonement. And therefore side by side with the
requirement of faith He has placed that of
baptism, giving us thus the synonym of
death and resurrection as the language in
which we must utter our confession of faith,
that we may never forget how we were redeemed.

Thus baptism is the divinely appointed
method of translating our obedience and faith
into the phraseology of our Lord's death and
resurrection. By it the disciple says to God,
not, "I have believed and obeyed the gospel,
therefore accept me;" but rather, "*It is
Christ that died, yea rather that is risen
again,*" [1] and I hereby declare my conformity

[1] Rom. viii. 34.

to his death, and my fellowship with his resurrection.

Noting more minutely the features of this apostolic ordinance, we shall see how it answers in every particular to the doctrine unfolded in previous chapters.

Here is first the *burial,* which confirms and seals our crucifixion in Christ. The Spirit declares " *The body is dead because of sin,*" [1] and the water opens now its mystic tomb to ratify that verdict. And how, as for a moment the prostrate form of the disciple disappears beneath the wave, is the whole solemn story of our death in Christ silently rehearsed! Here is no sparing or reprieving of our guilty nature. The inexorable purpose for which "*our old man was crucified with Him,*" is proclaimed without equivocation, "*that the body of sin might be destroyed.*" Judaism, that trial of man in the flesh, that system for his cleansing in his carnal state, had as its ordinance, circumcision, the typical rite of the *purification of the flesh.* But Christianity, starting upon the axioms that "The carnal mind is enmity against God," and that "They that are in the flesh cannot please God," [2] has a far different ordinance, even

---

[1] Rom. viii. 10.   [2] Rom. viii. 7, 8.

baptism, the typical rite of the *burial of the flesh,* in order to a better resurrection. Circumcision is " the putting away of the filth of the flesh ; "[1] baptism is " the putting off of the body of the sins of the flesh." [2] Therefore by this confession do we not only, as Edward Irving expresses it, "sign the death-warrant of our natural man which has been issued from the court of heaven," but we sign it literally with the " *sign of the cross ;* " the similitude of our Lord's death being the appointed and permanent vehicle of this confession, that so we may be constantly reminded not only that we must die to sin in order to live to God, but except we die *with Him* we cannot live with Him.

And can those who realize the greatness of those two dangers which are always threatening the Church, namely, a bloodless moralism on the one hand, and a spiritless ceremonialism on the other, be too grateful for the *form* of this ordinance which the Spirit has thus fixed? Substitute, as has been done, the sprinkling or pouring of water upon the person, for burial in the water ; thus let the *cleansing* only of the soul be signified

[1] 1 Pet. iii. 21. [2] Col. ii. 11.

in the rite, with no symbolic designation
of the method of that cleansing, death in
Christ. It is easy for the moralist now to
use the ordinance without ever having his
mind turned to the sacrifice of Calvary. Aye,
desiring not to see that sacrifice which means
death to the carnal man, he comes readily to
view the rite as a kind of Christian circumcision, marking the sanctifying of human nature, and bringing that into covenant with
God. And so, "as many as desire to make a
fair show in the flesh" will readily be con-
strained to adopt it, when both their heart and
their flesh would cry out against that baptism
into Christ's death which marks the crucifying and putting off of the old man. And
on the other hand how easily the idea of mystical efficacy becomes attached to the element
of water, unless the form of its use be such as
to carry the thought immediately and certainly to Christ crucified and dead. How
vitally important then that "form of doctrine" prescribed by the Scriptures, namely,
the sacramental burial, which, while it so distinctly signifies our union with Him "who
came by water," as distinctly adds the saving
clause, "*not by water only, but by water and
blood.*"

As we have intimated already, such a seal
of doom to the natural man will not be likely
to find much favor in this world. Why should
it ? It is the cross translated into symbol,
and the cross gets little human approbation.
The old offense and ignominy lurk even in its
shadow. Doubtless many a true believer has
turned back to circumcision from finding how
much deeper the gospel cuts than the law ;
and doubtless many another, who has gone
down with Christ into the mystic grave,
would have started back affrighted had he
realized all that he was showing forth.

But sorrow can have no place at this tomb
if we stop to consider how much is put off in
this putting off of our old man ; how the sin
that roots itself in that nature, the curse that
clings to that nature, and the condemnation
that rests upon that nature, are all swallowed
up in the sepulchre of Jesus Christ. The
cross condemns and brings death indeed, but
just beyond is the tomb where the condemnation is buried, and the death is swallowed
up in victory. "So I saw in my dream," says
Bunyan, "that just as Christian came up with
the cross, his burden loosed from off his
shoulders and fell from off his back, and be-

gan to tumble, and so continued to do *till it
came to the mouth of the sepulchre, when it
fell in, and I saw it no more.*"   And does not
this word, "I saw it no more," answer the
deepest note in the longing and groaning of
our sin-burdened humanity?   That Christian
cry, "Who shall deliver me from the body of
this death?" and that heathen cry embodied
in the fable of Lethe, whose waters of forgetfulness the dead are ever thirsting to drink
that they may enter into rest, are strangely
akin in this, — that it is the pain of an ach-
ing conscience, the sighing for ease from the
sting of sin, that is told alike in each.   And
where have these cries been answered but in
those sacramental waters, which in a figure
are at once the grave where the body of sin is
buried, and the river of forgetfulness where
bygone guilt is overwhelmed and its memory
swallowed up?   And when was ever God's
ancient promise, "Their sins and their iniqui-
ties I will remember no more," written in so
large letters as here?   Not surely in that law
that "stood in divers washings;"[1] for in that
there was "a remembrance again made of
sins every year."[2]   Not in that pseudo-gos-

[1] Heb. ix. 10.   [2] Heb. x. 3.

pel which places our hope in some cleansing
or betterment of human nature ; for in that,
hope dies, and bitter memories awake with
every fresh reviving of the evil principle.
But here is found an ordinance that says to
the believer " no condemnation," and " no
more conscience of sins."

 Say not then with a Romish Father,[1] that
" *The true penitent never forgives himself.*"
Say rather that he is one who has learned to
see in the grave of his Lord the burial of all
his sins, with their burning remembrances,
their bitter accusations, and their stinging re-
proaches, and so, entering into God's thought
concerning him, has learned to forgive himself in God's forgiveness of him. " Blessed
is he whose transgression is forgiven, *whose
sin is covered.*" " Blessed is the man to whom
the Lord imputeth not iniquity."

 And if there is a signing of the death-warrant of the natural man in this rite, there is
just as clearly the making over of a quit-
claim upon him by a satisfied law. For when
did the law ever pursue a culprit into his
grave ? To have died with Christ is to have
died to the law.[2] No avenger of blood can

[1] J. H. Newman.   [2] Rom. vii. 4.

pursue his victim within the guarded pre-
cincts of this city of refuge, the sepulchre of
Jesus. And to the fact of the believer's having entered here, the water is a perpetual witness. "I buried him with Christ," it says.
"I rolled my wave like a stone against the
door of his sepulchre. I set the seal of the
new covenant inscribed with the triune name
upon his tomb." And so every taunt of a
suspicious conscience, and every rising terror
of a broken commandment, is silenced.

If now it seems to any believer that he can
afford to lose the letter of this commandment
because forsooth "the letter killeth," it may
appear upon deeper reflection that this is just
the reason why he needs it. Confidence in
the flesh, and bondage to the law, are enemies
that we may rejoice to have killed ; and if
the letter of baptism can show them to our
faith as cut off and utterly destroyed in the
grave of Christ, it has done a blessed work
for us. Oh, would that all seekers after peace
might discover this — that there can be no
entrance into "the power of Christ's resurrection," except through conformity to his
death. Would that the tomb of Jesus might
be seen to be as it is, the only shelter from

the law, the only stronghold from the perse-
cutions of conscience. Then, the preciousness
of the doctrine being discovered, the preciousness of the symbol would be felt. And
how would they who have learned to say " I
am crucified with Christ," also

> " Joy to undergo
> This *shadow* of his cross sublime,
> This remnant of his woe."

But the buried form is raised up again from
the water in the likeness of Christ's resurrection. It should remain submerged, if Christ
be not risen. As it is, the momentary disap-
pearance from sight, and the brief suspension
of the breath, vividly suggests that fearful
doom which were ours in such a case. But
no sooner is the " *buried with Him in baptism* " spoken, than the " *Now is Christ risen
from the dead*" is answered and echoed back
by the joyful announcement, " *wherein also
ye are risen with Him through the faith of
the operation of God which hath raised Him
from the dead.*" [1] Blessed is he who, now
looking into the grave where he was buried
with Christ, sees what God sees, what the
angels see, the winding sheet of Adam's

[1] Col. ii. 12.

curse put off from him and folded up forever,
and the linen clothes of a legal righteousness
laid by themselves. And thrice blessed is he
who hears concerning himself the glad announcement, " He is not here, but is risen,"
and so is enabled to go forth in the joy of
the resurrection, to " walk in newness of life."
And this is what the Spirit by the water as
well as by the word would certify to us, — our
standing in union with our risen Head beyond the executed sentence of an injured law,
our complete security in Him, and our right
and duty to rejoice evermore in this grace.

The value of the ordinances is in their
power of bringing truth within the apprehension of all our senses, physical and spiritual.
Thus do they not only intensify our experience of doctrine, but they serve to put it
beyond further question, as that " which we
have heard, which we have seen with our
eyes, which our hands have handled of the
Word of Life." [1]

How vividly in the momentary chill and
darkness of the grave of baptism do we taste
his death who suffered for us all! And in the
exultant uprising, the quick recovery of the

[1] 1 John i. 1.

bated breath that follows, how fully do we seem to enter into the joyful experience of his quickening! So closely does the symbol thus press upon the reality, that Paul in that bold "Know ye not,"[1] seems to appeal to the believer's baptism as the *experience* of his Lord's death and resurrection, and as making it thus a subject of memory as well as of faith.

So by this memorial let the Christian know and remember that he has been quickened with Christ ; that henceforth his place is on resurrection ground, and he can fix it nowhere else without dishonoring his Lord. If, forgetting that his life is hid in the risen Christ, he is tempted to find it in Adam, let him hear all the floods of baptism lifting up their voice in rebuke, saying, "Why seek ye the living among the dead?" "Are ye so foolish, having begun in the Spirit, are ye now made perfect in the flesh?"[2] If, unmindful of his accomplished justification by faith, he yet lingers under the law, let him hear the bridal vow, which in baptism sealed him to the Lord Jesus, condemning him, "Ye are become dead to the law by the body of Christ, that *ye*

[1] Rom. vi. 3.   [2] Gal. iii. 2.

*should be married to another, even to Him
who is raised from the dead,* that ye should
bring forth fruit unto God." Every return to
the law now as a ground of justification, is
treachery and infidelity to the Bridegroom of
the Church ; and any righteousness or trust
brought forth from it, is only the fruit of a
criminal and forbidden relationship.

But above all must this memory serve as a
most tender and pathetic plea for a holy walk.
Sin now takes on added guilt, that of criminal inconstancy. Its stain is of a darker hue,
falling on that resurrection mantle. Its offense is a " crucifying of the Son of God afresh
and putting Him to an open shame." And
so no possible dissuasion from sin can be so
strong as this. " Neither yield ye your members as instruments of unrighteousness unto
sin ; but yield yourselves unto God *as those
that are alive from the dead,* and your members as instruments of righteousness unto
God." [1]

If baptism is for our " assurance of faith,"
as the sign that we are risen with Christ
spiritually, it is equally for our " assurance of
hope," as the prophecy that we shall rise

[1] Rom. vi. 13.

bodily at the last day.[1]   Has not a strange
apathy crept over the Church respecting this
her most glorious hope?   From Christ, who
spoke that first word of comfort to the bereaved, " Thy brother shall rise again," to the
Apostle who consoled the Thessalonian Christians with that confident " If we believe that
Jesus died and rose again, even so them also

---

[1] This truth is drawn out with great justness and force in
the following words of Dean Goulburn : " There can be no
doubt that baptism, when administered in the primitive and
most correct form, is a divinely constituted emblem of bodily resurrection.   And it is to be regretted that the form of
administration unavoidably (if it be unavoidably) adopted in
cold climates should utterly obscure the emblematic significance of the rite, and render unintelligible to all but
the educated, the Apostle's association of burial and resurrection with the ordinance.   Were immersion, which is the
rule of our Church in cases where it may be had without
hazard to the health, universally practiced, this association
of two at present heterogeneous ideas would become intelli-
gible to the humblest.   The water, closing over the entire
person, would then preach of the grave which yawns for
every child of Adam, and which one day will engulf us all
in its drear abyss.   But that abyss will be the womb and
seed plot of a new life.   Animation having been for one instant suspended beneath the water, a type this of the interruption of man's energies by death, the body is lifted up
again into the air by way of expressing emblematically the
new birth of resurrection." — *Bampton Lectures*, 1850.   Ox-
ford edition, p. 18.

which sleep in Jesus will God bring with Him," [1] this was the one blessed assurance with which primitive Christianity sought to dissipate the gloom of death. We dwell so much on the present joy of our dead who have gone to Christ, that we forget the joy that yet remains when God shall bring them with Him. But it is then only that death will be robbed of its sting and the grave of its victory. It is the resurrection that gives us back our beloved, looking and speaking as they were wont; that gives us back our bodies parted from us awhile, but endeared to us by the very sorrows we have borne in them; and that restores us wholly to the lost image of God, in which we were created, by making us to awake in the likeness of Christ, new created. Hence the eagerness of that waiting for the redemption of the body in which the whole creation shares.

As our whole nature, body, soul, and spirit, died in Adam, so must our whole nature, body, soul, and spirit, be made alive in Christ before our blessedness can be complete. And if we are in the Lord, our physical restitution is assured to us with equal certainty

[1] 1 Thess. iv. 14.

with our spiritual. For not only is it true
that "he that is joined to the Lord is one
spirit," but equally that we are members of
his *body*, of his flesh, and of his bones."
But as the Head is, so must be the members.
And they who, once unclothed by sin, have
now put on Christ by baptism, have thereby,
according to St. Bernard's fine saying, " had
two garments bestowed upon them : the one,
the *righteousness* of Christ, with which they
are already clothed in the joy and peace of
redeemed souls ; and the other, the *immortality* of Christ, with which they are yet to be
clad in the glory and incorruptibility of redeemed bodies."

That the hope of such a consummation
may not die out of the Church — as, alas !
what hope may not when her heart has
turned away from her Lord, and her eyes
from watching for his appearing — the Spirit
has not only reiterated it in scores of texts,
but enshrined it in this rite as in "a statuary
of truth which may endure though the pictur-
ing and writing of it should be effaced."

And let it be noted that of all the types
that have been employed to bring this hope
vividly to the Christian mind, not one ex-

cepting baptism is adequate to the reality.
Of a general resurrection which the Scriptures foretell, we see tokens and similitudes
all about us in nature, — in the flower, springing up from the seed which has fallen into
the earth and died ; in the morning, opening
the vast grave of night, and summoning a
sleeping world to rise and meet the sun " as
he cometh forth as a bridegroom from his
chamber ; " in the springtide, calling the
earth from the tomb of winter, loosing her
shroud of snow, and clothing her with renewed life and beauty ; in all these there are
joyful parables and pledges of a resurrection.
But the flower fades and dies, the morning
sinks again into the embrace of night, and
the earth lies down once more in the sepulchre of winter ; and so, alas ! these symbols
only mock the hope they have kindled in the
soul.   But while we are asking sorrowfully,
" Is there no resurrection that is exempt from
death ? " we turn to this ordinance of Christianity.   " Risen with Christ," it says ; and
then adding, " knowing that Christ being
raised from the dead *dieth no more, death
hath no more dominion over him*," [1] bids us

---

[1] Rom. vi. 9.

likewise reckon ourselves to be alive with Him in the same resurrection. Thus this symbol of the gospel carries a promise and a benediction which are committed to no symbol of nature. "Blessed and holy is he that hath part in the first resurrection ; *on such the second death hath no power.*" [1]

To such salutary uses, and for the declaration of such blessed hopes, was the ordinance of baptism appointed. It holds conspicuously before our minds the truths that are most vital to our assurance and comfort in the Lord Jesus Christ. To each believer, on his profession of faith, and to the whole church beholding, it presents a sensible image of the dying of the Lord Jesus and his rising again, and thus seeks to form the Christian heart and life according to the pattern received from God.

Were it only a form of ecclesiastical registration, it might perhaps be counted among the non-essentials of Christianity. But as the divine emblem through which faith apprehends our union with the dead and risen Redeemer, and by which the Spirit solemnly reminds us of our engagement to die daily to

[1] Rev. xx. 6.

sin in the mortifying of all unholy passions
and desires, and to walk in newness of life by
abiding in Christ, how shall we not most ten-
derly urge it upon all who love our blessed
Lord ?   Rather, how shall we not ourselves
most earnestly seek to preserve its integrity
and illustrate its beauty by reflecting it in a
consecrated and self-denying life ?   For we
cannot forget that it is an unsanctified life
that constitutes the worst perversion of this
rite.   The type may be perfect; but if the
impress with which it was meant to stamp a
life is blurred with inconsistencies and distorted by habitual sin, its perfection will not
appear.   For the seal is judged by its signature.

"Grant, O Lord, that as we are baptized
into the death of thy blessed Son our Saviour
Jesus Christ, so by continual mortifying of
our corrupt affections, we may be buried with
Him ; and that through the grave and gate of
death we may pass to our joyful resurrection,
for his merits who died and was buried and
rose again for us, thy Son Jesus Christ our
Lord.   Amen."

V. LIFE IN CHRIST.

✠

Therefore if any man be in Christ, he is a new creature.   2 *Cor.* v. 17.

I live, yet not I, but Christ liveth in me; and the life which I now live in the flesh I live by the faith of the Son of God, who loved me and gave Himself for me.   *Gal.* ii. 20.

Your life is hid with Christ in God. When Christ, who is our life, shall appear, then shall ye also appear with him in glory.   *Col.* iii. 3, 4.

✠

V.

LIFE IN CHRIST.

ITH what life do they come forth
from baptism, who have put on
Christ ? Even with that twofold life
of which baptism is the seal and the foreshadowing, — the crucified life of the first
Adam, and the risen life of the second Adam.

In a deeper sense than he meant it, is that
striking utterance of Lacordaire true, — " *The
Church is born crucified.*" For not only as
born of the Spirit has she been brought into
fellowship with the sufferings of Christ ; but
as born of water she has been stamped with
the cross of Christ, the birth-mark of her redemption, to be worn till death. And being
" begotten again unto a lively hope by the
resurrection of Jesus Christ from the dead,"
she has also the new and glorified life of her
Lord.

The prescribed course of Christian growth

and development then is exactly according to that type of doctrine to which we have been committed in baptism. " *Ye are dead,*"[1] is the doctrinal statement of the believer's status before the law. " *Mortify therefore your members which are upon the earth,*" is the practical inference to be worked out in holy living. "*Ye are risen with Christ,*"[1] is the other side of the same doctrinal statement. " *Seek those things which are above,*" is the corresponding exhortation to practical holiness. And so we see the truth of the axiom of a former chapter, that Christian experience is the making real in ourselves what is already true for us in Christ.

Of Jesus we might almost say that He never wholly ceases to be anything that He has once been ; there is such an unchanging permanency and vitality in every event of his redemption. Of the believer who is in Him, this is certainly true. He is one that not only *has died* with Christ, but one who in that very fact is bound to "*die daily* " with Him so long as he is in the flesh. He is one who not only has been made a "*new creature*" in Christ, but one whose inward man is

[1] Col. iii. 1, 6.

"*renewed* day by day." And so the cross
and the resurrection extend their influence
and exert their power over the Christian's
entire earthly history.

Of the twofold life in which this twofold
experience is carried on, let us consider a
moment.

We cannot regard it as a double phase of
one and the same life, but rather as the manifestation of two distinct natures, one of
which we derive from Adam, and the other
from Christ: natures which mingle and in-
terpenetrate indeed in the same soul, as air
and moisture occupy the same space in the
sky, but between which there can be no unity
of life. "*That which is born of the flesh is
flesh.*" The degenerate seed can only reproduce itself. It holds no germs or possibili-
ties of a divine life. "*That which is born of
the Spirit is spirit.*" The seed of God can
unfold only in the life of God, and through
all its endless reproductions, it is still "*the
incorruptible seed.*" So that while in the
Scriptures we have several distinct enumera-
tions of the fruits of the flesh and the fruits
of the Spirit, we never find the mention of
such an anomaly as a natural grace or a spir-

itual imperfection, the offspring of the two in
their amalgamation. Aye, more. Not only
is there no possible community of life between these two, but an irreconcilable enmity. "For the flesh lusteth against the
spirit, and the spirit against the flesh, and
these are contrary the one to the other." [1]

Here, in this awakened antagonism of
grace and nature, is the sword which Christ's
coming brings to every soul, — a sword which,
like that of the old crusader, proves upon in-
spection to be only the cross changed from a
symbol of faith into a weapon of conquest,
and which we must take up daily in following
Christ. For the old nature, though judged
and condemned and deposed in the death of
Christ, is forever revolting against its sentence, and struggling to regain its lost su-
premacy. And the new man from above, is
set to no less a task than his total overthrow
and reduction.

In the seventh of Romans we see the battle in progress between these two ; we watch
the advance and retreat of the forces of each.
Now we hear the groan of the wounded, " O,
wretched man that I am ; " and now, clear

[1] Gal. v. 17.

and strong above the conflict, we catch the shout of assured victory, — " I thank God through Jesus Christ." But it is a victory yet delayed. For the battle closes with both antagonists still alive and hostile. " So with my *mind* I myself serve the law of God, but with the *flesh* the law of sin."

And yet, though there can be no truce to this conflict this side the grave, there can be no doubt as to its ultimate issue. " Old Adam is too strong for young Melancthon," said the Reformer. *But he is not too strong for Christ*, and it is Christ that is in us, and we in Him. The very defeats of the believer therefore are victories, since, driven back from the outposts of self, a retreat into Christ becomes inevitable. Not as those who go to this warfare at their own charges, and carry it on from their own resources, does he con-tend. That is but Adam against Adam ; the natural man attempting to conquer himself ; a conquest which must always end in failure. He who is in Christ fights *from* victory in his very attempt to fight *for* victory. And therefore he is never so strong as when, from some fierce sortie upon the flesh, he retires into his fortress, confessing with renewed

humility that the Lord is his refuge and his
strength.

If the life of the believer were a unit, the
natural man improved merely, the old Adam
renewed and put in better dress, would there
not be something more than a paradox, —
would there not be a hopeless contradiction
in those words of the Apostle Paul, "When
I am weak then am I strong"?   One cannot
even by a figure be in two opposite conditions at the same time.   And within the
same sphere and in the same subject it is
hardly possible that strength should find its
highest perfection in weakness.   But this
contradiction vanishes when we read the
words in the light of that true expression of
the believer's nature, — "*I live, yet not I, but
Christ liveth in me.*"   There are two *I's* now,
if we may say so ; the positive and the negative, — the one from earth, and the other from
heaven.   The first has his name as well as
his nature, from the Head of the race, man,
one in Adam ; the second derives both his
name and his nature from the Head of the
Church, Christian, *one in Christ.*   And these
two, at present dwelling together, are yet
constantly at war ; the weakness and defeat

of the one always equivalent to the strength
and conquest of the other.

Will some one take up the proverb then
against the doctrine: "A house divided
against itself shall fall"? And so it must.
"We know that our earthly house of this tabernacle shall be dissolved." And this is our
victory. For thus only can this troublesome
tenant, the carnal man, be ejected, and we,
ceasing our self-conflicts and mortifications,
enter into that "building of God, that house
not made with hands, eternal in the heavens."
Meanwhile the believer's whole care and
striving must be directed to this end, the
causing of the house of Adam to wax weaker
and weaker day by day, and the house of
Christ to wax stronger and stronger.

Thus we see that the development of the
Christian towards perfection lies always in
these two opposite directions : the subjecting,
repressing, and mortifying of the natural man
on the one hand ; the nourishing, developing,
and renewing of the spiritual man on the
other.

Let us consider these two duties in detail.

The first is not, as many seem to deem it,
self-crucifixion, something to be begun and

7

carried on by ourselves and in ourselves.
Nay, it is the crucifixion which the believer
has undergone in Christ's person actualized,
prolonged, and reiterated in his own person.
As it is the office of faith to bring us into
doctrinal relationship to our Lord's dying, so
it is the office of love and obedience to bring
us into experimental relationship to it. For
deep as is the mystery, and as far below the
soundings of ordinary Christian consciousness, there is such a thing as realizing
Christ's death, and making it our own. We
know that even two human souls may have
become so identified by mutual love and the
fellowship of common suffering, that one is
made a sharer in the other's death. What a
touching illustration of this we have in the
lament of Eugénie de Guérin over the death
of her idolized brother! " My soul lives in a
coffin. Oh, yes, buried, interred with thee,
my brother. Just as I used to live in thy life,
I am dead in thy death, dead to all happiness,
all hope below."   .

Doubtless this is the expression of what
was sadly real to the heart of her who uttered
the words ; but not more so than that confession of a divine kindredship in suffering

which Paul makes, when he declares that
the world is crucified unto him, and he unto
the world, and that he is "always bearing
about in his body the dying of the Lord
Jesus," — statements so deep in their suggestion of spiritual intimacy as to make it seem
almost as though his very consciousness had
become identified with that of his Lord.

But while there may be something in this
which few can hope to imitate or even comprehend, there is also that which is very plain
and practical. The mortifying of the flesh,
the daily subduing of its sinful affections and
lusts, the bringing of the whole body under the
dominion of the cross, is not this most vital
to the believer's growth in holiness? For
our *justification*, the crucifixion ended indeed
in Christ; but for our *sanctification*, it must
be prolonged and perpetuated in ourselves.
Besides his heritage of peace in the death of
Jesus, every faithful disciple recognizes another legacy, even "*that which is behind in
the afflictions of Christ,*" [1] and which he is "to
fill up in his flesh for his body's sake, which
is the Church." And this spiritual birthright
he is never to part with. What a fearful
offense then is his who makes the cross a

[1] Col. i. 24.

reprieve for the flesh instead of an instrument for its subjection, who reasons that because Christ has suffered in the flesh, therefore he may live without suffering in the flesh. Quite contrary is this to the Scripture doctrine. " Forasmuch, then, as Christ hath suffered in the flesh, *arm yourselves likewise with the same mind.*"[1] " The saint, as having been judged in the person of Christ, and knowing that Christ for him has borne the cross, follows on by that cross, to judge and mortify all that he finds in himself still contrary to his Lord. The flesh is contrary to that Holy One ; the flesh in him therefore must die."[2] Its perverse affections must suffer daily denial ; its cries for unholy indulgence must be answered with stern refusals ; its high thoughts and proud ambitions must be made to endure the cross and despise the shame of constant humiliations. So that if we embrace the cross only that we may be borne above the reach of pain and loss, that human nature may be spared instead of slain by it, we have learned Christ but imperfectly. Not by thrusting away the atonement alone, but by " minding earthly things," living for

[1] 1 Pet. iv. 1.   [2] Andrew Jukes.

them instead of being dead to them, do we place ourselves among the "enemies of the cross of Christ."[1] While therefore the voice of the merely superficial disciple is, " Let us go to Christ that we may escape suffering and death," the voice of the true disciple is ever that of Thomas, " Let us go *that we may die with Him.*"

Die with Him ! Both suffering and death, while they are the common and inevitable heritage of the race, may in the believer's case be so linked into union with the cross and passion of his Lord, that they shall in a certain sense be transformed from inflictions into sacrifices. If he joyfully puts his free-will into the dispensations of God's sovereign will, and thus takes up the cross instead of enduring it like Simon the Cyrenean by compulsion, he has become an offerer instead of a victim, prolonging in his own body the sufferings of his Lord whereby he is perfected. He has taken chastisement out of the hand of blind adversity, and made it an instrument of self-discipline. So that the disciple may find his needed cross without imposing self-appointed austerities upon himself, even in

[1] Phil. iii. 18.

the willing acceptance of that which is against
the natural will, but which God sends upon
him in labors and in humiliations, in sickness
and in trials, in privations and in death.

But how hard it is for Christians to learn
this lesson, that salvation is not according to
the will of the flesh, but contrary to it ; not
from death, but *through* it.   The Master's
word is, "He that loseth his life for my sake
shall find it."   And yet when called to endure this loss in giving up some dearest joy
or some "other self" according to the flesh,
we wonder and demur, perhaps count ourselves forsaken of our Master, and take up
Martha's plaintive cry, "Lord, if thou hadst
been here, my brother had not died."   To
which Jesus only answers, "I am the Resurrection and the Life."   Not to give us im-
munity from death, but to lead us through it
to life ; not to save us from the cross, but to
bring us by way of it to a blessed crown, is
our Lord's purpose concerning us.

Were this crucial test of discipleship, the
willing surrender of self in all its forms, its
will, its pleasure, its righteousness, insisted
on in the Church as it is in the gospel, we
fear it would be found that the offense of the

cross had not ceased. But on the other hand, were all who are Christ's to show the holy triumph there is in giving up all for Him, the deep joy in being partakers of his sufferings, the blessed life that comes through daily death in Him, how powerfully would the ancient glory of the cross be vindicated.

For the love of our Lord, then, let not the *doctrine* of the cross, and the *endurance* of the cross be separated in our lives, that so we may forsooth be saved *by* crucifixion and yet saved *from* crucifixion.

Is that instrument of our Redeemer's suffering more beautiful to Him, as when carved in wood or stone it stands as a symbol of faith, or as when wrought into an ordinance it serves as a sacrament of allegiance, than when, reproduced in a mortified life, it is made the ornament of a meek and quiet spirit? To trace its outlines in a self-surrendered will; to show its transfigured form in the daily yielding of our reluctant flesh to hard service for our Lord; to exhibit its marks in a wounded but unresisting pride; to show a carnal mind always delivered up to death by it for Christ's sake, this will be the disciple's life-long work, if he truly understand his calling.

To some this may seem a hard doctrine,
and to others a contemptible one. Even
while we write we seem to hear such words
as *asceticism* and *pietism* whispered against
it. But we can only ask, Has the old man
grown better during these eighteen hundred
years, so that, whereas the primitive saints
were to put him off with his deeds, we may
be allowed to spare him and indulge him?
Has the body of the flesh become so kind
and so helpful to the Spirit, that we have no
need, like Paul, to keep it under and bring it
into subjection lest we be castaways? If
there were no answer from revelation to this
question, there is one from universal human
experience. None has ever yet found un-
tempered self-gratification compatible with
strong spiritual growth. None has ever yet
discovered how to give nature all it asks,
without defrauding grace. Whether it be
the "lust of the flesh" restraining the body
from chastened self-control; or the "lust of
the eyes" withdrawing the vision from single
contemplation of Jesus Christ; or the "pride
of life" lifting up the heart in vain glory, the
testimony of experience is at one with that
of Scripture, that "fleshly lusts war against

the soul." Never can they be turned into allies; never will they consent to be mere neutrals in the field.

Surely, therefore, the loyal believer will not count it treason against human nature to take up arms against himself at the call of Christ, if it is by self-subjection that the kingdom of God is to be set up in him. Nor will suffering be deemed an anomaly after the sufferings of Jesus finished for us, nor death a redundancy after his dying endured for us, if the life of God within the soul only reaches its triumph in the casting out of the life of nature. Rather will he rejoice to carry on a warfare which Jesus Christ begun, not ended for us; and to bend his will to a necessity which He has sanctified, not abolished for us.[1]

But as we have intimated, there is another element in the Christian life that forms the exact counterpart to this which we have been considering; namely, that abiding in Christ, and that growing up in all things into Him

---

[1] "Jesus Christ has not abolished our sufferings and our mortality, but He has made them what they never could have been without Him, a bitter dew which develops and matures in our souls the blessed germ of faith." — *Vinet.*

who is the Head, which is the end and object of this withdrawing from self and this
mortifying in all things of our members which
are on the earth. A negative process is not
adequate to accomplish a positive result.
And no amount or kind of self-denial can
make one holier, unless this be the means of
bringing him into more intimate fellowship
with Christ. Every retreat from the life of
the flesh must be followed by a deeper entering into the life of the Spirit. Self-denial is,
according to its degree, a parting company
with Adam that we may not walk after the
flesh ; but prayer and faith and love and obedience must accompany, as the means of
joining ourselves more entirely to Christ, and
of abiding in Him, that we may so walk even
as He walked.

Now is it not painfully common for Christians to rest satisfied with the fact that they
have life in the risen Jesus, without any strivings for higher degrees in that life ? Just as
we are prone to end our crucifixion with
Christ's cross, we are prone to end our seeking of those things which are above, in the
fact that we are risen with Christ. " He that
hath the Son hath life" indeed. But let him

not forget that his blessing is only begun in
this possession, since Jesus' work is only begun in this gift. " I am come that they
might have life, and *that they might have it
more abundantly.*" The seed of God must
not abide alone. The soil of human nature
has been furrowed to no purpose by chastisement, and softened without use by mortification, if this kernel of divine life be not
thereby helped to reproduce itself in more
abundant harvest. Life begets life continually. Nay more, the life of God must be
daily replacing within the soul what death
has taken away, filling each void made by
self-denial with some positive blessing, and
causing every spot from which a natural
affection has been uprooted, to spring up
with some divine affection.

Herein, if we mistake not, has been the
radical defect in the whole system of monas-
tic penance and discipline. Its *destructive*
work has far exceeded its *constructive.* It
has not builded into the rents which it has
made in human nature with a better material,
nor been careful to heal over the deep wounds
which it has inflicted upon the carnal man
with a new growth from the Spirit. Hence

the type of life which it has generally presented has been that of ever increasing brokenness rather than that of growing whole-
ness of being, and its ideal saints have been
those most thoroughly uprooted and torn
away from nature, rather than those most
truly "*rooted and built up in Christ.*"

But what will it profit one to lose the whole
world, if he does not gain his own soul? gain
it in that only way in which it can be gained,
by bringing it more and more into communion with the life of Christ? As it was the
supreme mission of Jesus to give eternal life,
so it is the supreme calling of the believer to
appropriate that life. And for this something more than an empty heart is demanded.
There must be a hungering and a thirsting
heart, a believing and a praying heart — a
heart ever longing after God, and seeking to
know more of God.

Self-denial is of the nature of self-discovery,
since it enables one to look more deeply into
human nature through the very void it has
refused to fill. But "*know thyself*" is not
the gospel precept for the attainment of eternal life. "This is life eternal, *that they might
know Thee, the only true God, and Jesus*

Christ whom Thou hast sent." And how ".know," except by that daily acquainting ourselves with Him which comes through faith and prayer, through a diligent searching of the Scriptures, through a constant walking in the Spirit, and through a strenuous exercise of vital godliness? Every duty indeed of the Christian has a direct relation to this result.

Communion, the constant partaking of the divine life through the appetites and organs which that life has supplied, is the knowing of God through identification with the nature of God. As between man and man, thought is the medium of life, and the words of intimate conversation serve to transmit the subtle essence of intelligence, affection, and feeling, from one to another; so between the renewed soul and God. Spiritual converse is the means to a community of spiritual life. But as in the one case, so in the other, such knowledge is possible only because of the possession of a common spirit. " For what man knoweth the things of a man, save the spirit of man which is in him ? Even so the things of God knoweth no man but the Spirit of God." And this spirit in the believer is the interpreter to God of his longings, making intercession for him with groanings that cannot be uttered, and the revealer to him of the things of Christ, which He taketh and showeth unto him.

And meditation serves the same end ; for from the devout contemplation of the character of Christ, his image is insensibly reproduced in the life of the believer. And so, as by communion one enters into fellowship with Jesus Christ, by meditation he enters into conformity to Him. And these two are the principal requisites to our attainment of the fullness of the stature of Christ, his life constantly imparted, and his character constantly reflected. Through the one, obedience tends more and more to become the spontaneous law of our being, and service the unconstrained fulfillment of God's word ; and through the other, likeness to the Lord Jesus grows more and more towards realized oneness with Him, while, "beholding as in a glass the glory of the Lord, we are changed into the same image from glory to glory, even as by the Spirit of the Lord." [1]

Now while we have said elsewhere that the

[1] 2 Cor. iii. 18.

negative process of self-mortification is not adequate to the positive result of conformity to Christ, the opposite is not true. Communion with Jesus is a certain means to the excommunication of sin. Growth in grace can never fail to promote the subjection of nature. If we have striven in vain to root out the tares which the enemy has sown in the heart, we may yet rejoice to know that they cannot endure the burning heat of Christ's unclouded presence. The offending eye which we have not succeeded in plucking out, we may yet so dazzle by a continued looking unto Jesus, that it shall be blind to its former allurements.

We shall not wait then till we have perfected our self-denial before we begin our growth into Christ. The two processes must ever be going on together. How striking the significance of that twofold exhortation of Paul so constantly repeated, "*Put ye off*" and "*Put ye on.*"

"Seeing that ye have put off the old man with his deeds, and have put on the new man."[1] This is the ideal saint, — the man in Christ whom God has fully justified. And

[1] Col. iii. 9, 10

the whole course of the Christian life must consist in the transferring of this ideal into the actual, in progressive sanctification. So must we be ever putting off all that belongs to the old man, — " Anger, wrath, malice, blasphemy, filthy communication out of the mouth ; " and putting on all that belongs to the new man, — " an heart of pity, kindness, lowliness of mind, meekness, long suffering, and above all things love, which is the bond of perfectness." [1]

If there is something painful in such a process, this life-long clothing and unclothing of the soul, we know that it will have an end. When death shall have disrobed us of our mortality, we shall cease from our putting off, and fold up and lay aside for the last time that garment which we have striven in vain to keep unspotted from the world. And when we awake in the morning of our redemption, our putting on will be also consummated, even " when this corruptible shall have put on incorruption, and this mortal shall have put on immortality."

[1] Col. iii. 14.*

VI. STANDING IN CHRIST.

8

✠

Of Him are ye in Christ Jesus, who of God is made unto us . . . . righteousness. *1 Cor.* i. 30.

There is therefore now no condemnation to them that are in Christ Jesus. *Rom.* viii. 1.

Wherein He hath made us accepted in the Beloved. *Eph.* i. 6.

And ye are complete in Him. *Col.* ii. 10.

✠

VI.

IF the Christian life on earth must be one of perpetual conflict, it is not therefore one of perpetual uncertainty. For though the believer's practical sanctification, or what he is in himself, may be the subject of constant solicitude and intense anxiety, yet his justification, or what he is in Christ, is something entirely aloof and detached from all the vicissitudes and fluctuations of Christian experience. It neither rises nor falls with the tide of feeling. It knows nothing of degrees. Christ being the standard by which it is gauged, it becomes absolute and without the possibility of change, since He is "the same, yesterday, to-day, and forever."

Our communion may be subject to sad alternations of warmth and coldness; our love may burn strongly to-day and feebly to-

morrow. But that does not change our real
standing before God. We cannot now be in
a state of justification and now out of it.
Doubt and unfaithfulness may throw the
shadow back many degrees to-day on the
dial-plate of hope ; but God does not look at
that to determine our acceptance with Him.
He sees us only in the light of the true Sun
of righteousness, and that is "without varia-
bleness neither shadow of turning."

Is then the wandering son just as near, and
the faithless one just as dear, to the Father's
heart, as that son to whom He saith, " Thou
art ever with me, and all that I have is thine" ?
Nay. But he is none the less a son. For
sonship does not depend on fellowship, but
fellowship on sonship. An apostle of free
grace [1] in degenerate times wrote, " Beloved
John may have more of Christ's affection than
Philip, and a brighter crown than Philip, but
he cannot have more justification than Philip.
Because, though there are degrees in the affection and rewards of Christ, there can be
none in his justification. A man must either
have the whole or none at all ; must either be
justified from all things or be condemned."

[1] John Berridge.

A strong statement, indeed, and perhaps an incredible one to those who are enamored of the *discipline of uncertainty* as the only means of keeping the believer watchful. But it is not stronger certainly than that word of an older Apostle, " There is therefore now no condemnation to them which are in Christ Jesus."

And is it not well for us sometimes to go around to the God-ward side of the covenant, and from much and bitter self-condemnation, enter into God's judgment of us as it is in Christ ? Faith has its appointed rest as well as its prescribed labor, when from the week-day toil and conflict of working out our own salvation, we may enter into our chamber of peace in the Lord, and shutting our doors about us say, "Return unto thy rest, O my soul, *for the Lord hath dealt bountifully with thee*," — so bountifully, if we will remember it, that in our destitution of any satisfying right-eousness, Christ is of God "made unto us righteousness," and in our emptiness of all good, " of his fullness have all we received, and grace for grace."

Many will warn us of the peril of slothful-ness and vain confidence arising from such a doctrine; and we on our part must warn such of the danger alike of a feeble faith and futile works, arising from an unestablished assurance. If faith has no standing ground except what it wins for itself; no stronghold except what it is enabled to build from time to time by its own endeavors, it can have little comfort, and can make but few conquests. And God has not ordained the matter thus. He has put a greater attainment behind us, than the most ardent disciple dares to place immediately before himself, even completeness in the Lord Jesus.

And so from every fresh manifestation of our self-incompleteness, we may retreat under cover to this gracious assurance, "Ye are complete in Him." We may *sink into Christ* when we cannot rise to Him. And thus we shall be made strong and victorious through apparent defeat, as again and again —

> "The steps of Faith
> Fall on the seeming void and find
> The Rock beneath."

If now it be asked, How can it be true of imperfect, tempted, and failing believers that they are complete in Christ? we must find the answer in God's gracious judgment of them as revealed by the Spirit. From this it would appear that so far as the question of the Christian's acceptance and standing before a righteous law is concerned, God sees nothing from his throne but Christ Jesus alone and altogether. And since the believer is in Him and one with Him, he shares his place in the Father's heart, and unworthy as he is in himself, yet he may know without a doubt that he is "*accepted in the Beloved.*"

And what a blessed word is this, "*in the Beloved.*" In that voice that came from heaven, "This is my beloved Son, in whom I am well pleased," we may now hear God's approving sentence upon ourselves, as well as upon our Lord. For being in Christ, the beams of the eternal love falling upon Him must fall upon us as included in Him, thus embracing us, within the circle of the divine complacency. We cannot be loved of God apart from Christ. For the divine approval can only go out to that which is worthy, and who that ever walked the earth has been worthy, save One? Neither can we be condemned if we are in Christ. For the divine disapprobation can fall only upon what is sinful. And He is without sin. To be in Him, therefore, is to be loved of the Father, because it is to be in the very focus of the divine affection. To be in Him is also to love the Father, since it is to be in union with the only heart that loves supremely and perfectly.

Is not the occasion of much of our distrust and darkness to be found in the fact that we estimate ourselves by ourselves, "according to the measure of a man," instead of according to the measure of Christ? He is the true exponent of our standing before God. "As He is, so are we in this world." [1] He holds us in Himself, and presents us to the eye of the Father, bright in the shining vestments of his own righteousness, and rich with the dowry of his blood-bought merit. He is not a meditator of one but of two. He not only represents God to us in his own being, "the brightness of his glory and the express image of his person," but He represents us to God. We see God in Christ. God sees us in Christ. God was in Christ reconciling the world unto Himself. We in Christ are reconciled unto God. Never can we pray, "O Lord, look Thou upon *me;* preserve my soul, for *I* am holy." More and

[1] 1 John i. 18.

more shall we learn to take up and urge, with
all the energy of a self-ignoring faith, the cry,
" Behold, O God, our Shield, and look upon
the face of thine Anointed." And the even-
ness of our joy and the stability of our hope
depend upon our keeping our gaze fixed im-
movably upon that one Blessed Object upon
·which the Father's gaze is always fixed.

If we measure our hope solely by the clear-
ness with which Christ's likeness is reflected
in our own character and experience, we can
find little comfort. For our life is at best but
a dim and distorted mirror that can neither
hold nor reflect any perfect image. If, forgetting ourselves, we delight only in looking unto Jesus and tracing the lineaments
of his divine countenance, we shall not only
be ever growing into the same image from
glory to glory till we are sanctified ; but remembering that God contemplates us even
now in that image, we shall be able to rejoice
as those that are already justified.

Now, while such words as "justified from
all things," and "no condemnation," as ap-
plied to the believer, establish beyond a question both the fullness and the fixedness of
his pardon, do not the great mass of Chris-

tians regard it practically as lying along a
kind of sliding scale of frames and feelings
where it is depressed or elevated according
to the feebleness or intensity of our religious
comfort ; capable of variation, indeed, from
the zero point of almost total condemnation
to that of full acceptance ?

But we cannot forget that as God put the.
terms of salvation so high that we could not
of ourselves make them ; so He has put our
title-deeds to salvation so high that we may
not mar them, having hidden them " with
Christ in God." As " holy Rutherford " says,
" Unbelief may perhaps tear the copies of the
covenant which Christ hath given you ; *but
He still keeps the original in heaven with
Himself. Your doubts and fears are no part
of the covenant, neither can they change
Christ.*"

If Christ is the complete and only reason
of our acceptance, must there not be some
greater reason for our rejection than our
doubts and misgivings ? If " in Christ Jesus
we who sometimes were afar off are made
nigh," will it not take something more than
our distrust and despair to remove us far off
again, and set us among aliens and strangers ?

Let us speak with the deepest reverence on so tender a theme ; and put off the shoes of self-confidence from our feet as we tread upon this holy ground, and dwell upon this grace wherein we stand. And yet we may well beware lest God's faithfulness find us more skeptical than his severity. The deepest sense of unworthiness is nowise inconsistent with the highest confidence in God's full and perfect justification of us. And we may without contradiction join the confession of a weak faith and much guilty unbelief with the exulting confidence, "If we believe not, yet He abideth faithful ; He cannot deny Himself." [1]

We have already spoken of the temptation to reckon our standing with God by our sense of personal worthiness at any given time. But we have only to know that the righteousness of Christ is upon us by our union with Him, to be assured that the approval and blessedness which that righteousness can win for Him, it can win for us.

True, as John Bunyan says, "The righteousness is still *in Christ,* and not in us, even when we are made partakers of the benefit of

[1] 2 Tim. ii. 13.

it ; even as the wing and feathers still abide in the hen when the chickens are covered, kept, and warmed thereby." But that they who have put their trust under the shadow of his wing are covered and kept and warmed, is just what we are urging. Aye, so completely covered, that the storm of a violated law cannot reach them ; and so kept, that that wicked one toucheth them not ; and so warmed, that no death chill of the penalty of sin can come to them. And it is this fact, that our righteousness is not our own, that makes it possible for us to glory in it, joining to the confession, " *I know that in me, that is in my flesh, dwelleth no good thing,*"[1] that other, " *I knew a man in Christ, of such an one will I glory.*"[2]

Is there any more striking illustration of the total change of place and relationship which the Scriptures recognize as having taken place in the believer than is found in Paul's bold way of *dating back* to the natural state as " *when we were in the flesh* "?[3] To be in Christ is to be in the true *Anno Domini,* from whence we look back and see the whole time past of our lives lived in the flesh now

[1] Rom. vii. 18.   [2] 2 Cor. xii. 1.   [3] Rom. vii. 5.

ended at the cross ; and then in the risen
Christ all begun afresh in perfect blessing
and in the power of an endless life.

We sighed for the love of God before, but
could find no sense or assurance of it, because we could find nothing in us or upon
us which it could approve. But now we see
how as risen with Christ we have been borne
up into the favor of the Father and into the
full fruition of the prayer, "*that the love
wherewith Thou hast loved me may be in them
and I in them.*"

We sighed for better desires and a true
"hunger and thirst after righteousness."
But God has done better for us than we
knew how to ask or think. He has given us
both the hunger and its satisfaction, both the
new nature from the Lord and that which
that nature wants, righteousness in the Lord.
The law of entail which made us heirs in
Adam of what we most longed to be free
from, sin, and death by sin, now holds to
make us heirs in Christ of what we most
longed to possess, holiness and everlasting
life. "As is the earthy, such are they also
that are earthy, *and as is the heavenly, such
are they also that are heavenly.*"

And what shall be the influence of these truths upon our daily life? To make us use little heed, because we have such a plenitude of righteousness in Christ, to fulfill righteousness in ourselves? Nay, but do they not present us with the most powerful motive to purity that one can possibly have? In Christ our righteousness, we see not what we are excused from, but what we are pledged to. We understand ourselves only in Him, what we are in God's esteem, and not the less what we must be in our personal attainment.

In divine things as in common things we say that a noble life is impossible without a noble ideal. But what if that ideal be a holy Person, and He not One whom we have *set before ourselves*, but one whom we have *put on?* Ought we not to say that an unholy life should be impossible in such a case, since the ideal has become more than an incentive, it has become the sacred guarantee of an actual and realized perfection in ourselves?

And this is literally the case. Justification pledges a holy life on the part of him who receives it, just as truly as it pledges eternal life on the part of Him who gives it.

And much as we rejoice in that gracious decree wherein He has made us "accepted in the Beloved," we cannot forget that wrapped up in the same decree is that other purpose wherein "He also did predestinate us *to be conformed to the image of his Son.*"[1] So that it would seem that high views of saintship must tend inevitably to make one intensely eager for high attainments in saintship.

But what if it be said that the dwelling by faith in a position so much above our actually attained one, must end in our dwelling very little among the common every-day duties of practical life? No objection has been more strenuously urged than this. Yet doubtless the common experience of Christians is that it is far more difficult to rise betimes above the conflict and endeavor of hard practical service, into the rest of faith and the blessedness of assured justification in Christ, than having so risen to descend again. The Mount of Transfiguration is never so far removed from the plain of daily duty, that a few steps will not suffice to bring us back among the "much people" and within hearing of the

[1] Rom. viii. 29.

beseeching cry of those possessed of the evil spirit.

And more than this ; so far from tending to selfish isolation from the world and indifference to its sorrows, its needs, and its sins, communion with Christ ought to be and must inevitably be, if real, the means of bringing us into the deepest fellowship with human suffering. The righteousness of Christ can never be worn as a mere outer garment, which while it covers the soul neither touches it nor transforms it. Every putting on of the Lord Jesus must result more and more in having that *mind* in us which was also in Him ; and that mind is one which leads to humiliation, even unto death, for the sake of the lost. We cannot forget that the same Apostle who rested so absolutely in the righteousness of Christ for his own salvation, that he said, " I count all things but loss that I may win Christ, and *be found in Him not having mine own righteousness*," yet had so much of the mind of Christ respecting the salvation of others, that he said, " God is my witness how I long after you all *in the tender heart of Jesus Christ.*" [1]

[1] Phil. i. 8.*

We must remember that to be in Christ is not only to be in union with the divine nature, but also, because He is the Son of man as well as the Son of God, it is to be in truest union with human nature. We never get so near the heart of our sorrowing humanity, as when we are in communion with the heart of the man of sorrows. And if we have prayed for a "*heart baptized into a sense of all conditions,*" [1] let us know that we shall find the fullest answer to our prayer in realizing that baptism into Christ which we have already received, since "As many as have been baptized into Christ, have put on Christ, in *whom is neither Jew nor Greek, bond nor free, male nor female, but all are one in Christ Jesus.*" [2] Because He is the universal man, the man without a country, since belonging alike to all, and the man without exclusive kindredship, since finding his mother and his brethren in whomsoever the will of his Father is obeyed, union with Him must lift us, as nothing else can, above all respect of persons and into universal sympathies. Since, then, Christ is

[1] "I prayed to God," says George Fox, "that He would baptize my heart into a sense of all conditions, that so I might be able to enter into the needs and sorrows of all."

[2] Gal. iii. 27, 28.

not divided, we, having his righteousness upon
us, must have his heart within us. And having that heart, how shall we not follow whith-
ersoever it leads, even into all conditions and
into all needs that belong to our race?

And if a sense of his completeness in
Christ does not beget indifference or selfish-
ness in the believer's heart, it surely cannot
engender pride. For is not pride always
some form of self-consciousness? And it is
the very reverse of self-consciousness to know
that we are nothing in ourselves, and that all
our righteousness is in another. Or, to look
at the opposite of pride, can true humility
flourish except under the shadow of some
overtowering greatness? It is by being in
the all worthy One that we discover as nowhere else how unworthy we are, because of
the contrast which we are compelled constantly to behold.

Experiment has demonstrated that the most
brilliant light which human science can pro-
duce, when projected upon the disc of the sun,
is literal darkness in comparison. In Christ's
righteousness we discover the worthlessness
of our own, — how it not only can add nothing to the lustre of that which is as white as

the light, but would rather tarnish it if it were laid upon it. And so every contemplation of ourselves in the Perfect One must make self-righteousness cover its face, and pride shrink away abashed.

There will however be no fleeing away from the presence of the Lord on this account. With the deepest sense of guilt and unholiness, there will yet be a deathless clinging of the heart to Him whose moral glory has so humbled us. With the profound sense of unfitness to be in his righteousness, there will be connected an inward consciousness that it is the only shelter one can be in and live.

And if no sense of unworthiness can keep us from Jesus, no sense of worthiness ever can. For the Refuge of the sinner must ever also be the Refuge of the saint, — "the strong tower into which the *righteous* runneth and is safe."

The Lord may give us many a victory in our upward strivings towards perfection ; and He may add daily to our stature as we seek to grow up into Him who is our Head ; but when shall we get beyond the deep petition of that hymn which its author so worthily

styled *" a living and dying prayer for the
holiest believer in the world,"* —

> " Rock of Ages, cleft for me,
> *Let me hide myself in Thee"* ?

From our sin and from our righteousness
alike, from our evil deeds and from our good
deeds, from the rebukes of an upbraiding
conscience and from the flatteries of an easy
conscience, we shall ever need to fly unto that
name whereby we are called, — " *The Lord
our Righteousness."*

VII. PRAYER IN CHRIST.

✠

If ye abide in me, and my words
abide in you, ye shall ask what ye will,
and it shall be done unto you.

John xv. 7.

Verily, verily I say unto you, What=
soever ye shall ask the Father in my
name, He will give it you.

John xvi. 23.

✠

VII.

PRAYER IN CHRIST.

AMONG the richest privileges growing out of that divine union on which we have been meditating is that of prayer in the name of Jesus. Indeed, it is at once the most precious fruit of the Believer's life in Christ and the most powerful nourisher of that life — that by which it both holds and is held.

And yet it may be questioned whether to the mass of Christians the deepest thought of that thrice repeated promise of our Lord, "Verily, verily, I say unto you, Whatsoever ye shall ask the Father *in my name* He will give it you,"[1] is not a hidden thought — namely, that asking in the name of Christ is asking *in union with the Person of Christ.*"[2]

One common apprehension of the matter is certainly true, that the Christian is permitted

---

[1] John xvi. 23.   [2] Note J.

to use the credit of that " name which is above
every name " in making his request to God.
And this is indeed an inestimable privilege.
For we know even in human relations how
much of one's personal qualities and attributes his name carries with it ; how that he
who is permitted to use his patron's name is
thereby to a certain extent invested with that
patron's character, so that whatever commer-
cial or moral value belongs to it is for the
time made over to him and becomes a personal possession. But another quite as common view of the matter is certainly not true,
that any request, whatever its nature, needs
only to have the words " for Christ's sake "
attached to it to ensure an answer. Nay !
To pray in Christ's name is not ·to use his
name as a charm or talisman simply, as
though the bare repetition of it were all that
is required to open the treasures of infinite
grace. Let us not degrade this dearest
promise of our Lord into such a superstition
as that. The Jewish cabalists believed that
the pronunciation of certain magical words
engraved on the seal of Solomon would per-
form miracles. That was incantation. And
we in like manner make Christian incantation

of this sublimest privilege of the Gospel if we put such an interpretation as this upon Christ's words.

The name of Christ stands for Christ Himself. And to pray in the name of Christ is to pray in Christ, in the mind and spirit and will of Christ. "*If ye abide in me, and my words abide in you, ye shall ask what ye will, and it shall be done unto you.*"[1]

To' repeat a holy name is an easy thing ; but to attain that holy abiding in which there is such a perfect community of life with our true Vine, that it is as impossible for us to ask amiss as for the branch of the fig-tree to put forth the buds and flowers of the thorn, is, as we all confess, to reach the very highest ideal of discipleship. And yet on nothing short of this perfectness of union with our Lord has He predicated an unrestricted access to the treasuries of divine blessing. The same condition is affixed to each of the highest and most longed-for attainments of the Christian life, — sinlessness,[2] fruitfulness,[3] and prevalence in prayer ; namely, "*If ye abide in me.*" Our desires, like the bud upon the tree, are the most concrete and perfect expression

[1] John xv. 7.   [2] 1 John iii. 6.   [3] John xv. 5.

of ourselves. Just to the degree in which we
are living in the flesh shall we be gendering
"the desires of the flesh and of the mind,"
bringing them to God in our prayers, and fulfilling them in our lives. Just to the degree
in which we realize that blessed state, "I live,
yet not I, but *Christ liveth in me,*" will the
desires of the Spirit be forming within us, —
unfolding in prayers that are "unto God a
sweet savor of Christ," and maturing into
the fruits of righteousness and true holiness.
No mere selfish and earth-born desire can be
endued with power, simply by being christened
with that holy name. Nor can any longing towards God which has been truly begotten by the Spirit fail because the formula,
"*for Christ's sake,* may be wanting in its utterance. The secret of the Lord lies deeper
than this — even in that full intimate fellowship with Jesus wherein our wills are perfectly accordant with his will as touching the
thing we ask, and our desires an impulse of
his holy mind.[1] The circuit of grace is complete and unobstructed between the Father,
the Son, and the Spirit. If we wholly abide
in Christ we get into its open and ever free

[1] Note K.

currents, where all things are possible to us who believe, because all things are possible with God, with whom we are thus brought into full accord.

Has not a wide-spread skepticism grown up among Christians concerning the literalness of this great promise, "Whatsoever ye shall ask"— a limiting of God's faithfulness in giving, through an ignoring of that constant limitation to our receiving, namely, our want of unbroken communion with Christ?

It is indeed a promise wonderful in its breadth: "If ye shall ask anything in my name, I will do it."[1] But because none may have ever fully measured it in human experience, shall it therefore be narrowed or conditioned as a divine possibility? "Prayer," it has been said, "is so mighty an instrument that no one ever yet mastered all its keys. They sweep along the infinite scale of man's wants and God's goodness." And yet to be the perfect servant of Christ's will is to be the perfect master of prayer. To the touch of that will all its majestic octaves respond. "I know that thou hearest me always."[2] And if we attune our wills perfectly to this divine

[1] John xiv. 14.   [2] John xi. 42.

will, how shall not the Father with Him
freely give us all things! The answer to
prayer then is not contingent on the greatness or the smallness of the requests it con-
tains, but upon the impulse which prompts
them. If that impulse proceed from our own
will, the prayer is not in the name of Christ,
though it relate to his kingdom. For even
so great a request as the glory of God may
be made from a selfish motive. But when
the incitement to prayer is derived from an
inward divine operation, it is truly in the
name of the Lord, and must have its answer.
For it is then the effectual *inwrought* prayer
that availeth much.

Does this view suggest the question, What
need then of prayer, since its limits are so
circumscribed that to be genuine it must only
be the expression of what God worketh in us
to will and to desire? A question which
may be answered by two others. First, Does
the devout mind desire any larger range for
its petitions than the circle of the perfectly
wise and perfectly beneficent will of God?
To know that our Lord had put into our
hands a key which was entirely within the
control of our blind, imperfect, erring wills,

were to know our constant peril of opening
for ourselves some door of certain destruction.
Hence ought it not to be a ground of the
deepest comfort and security to the suppliant
praying in the spirit of adoption, that he has a
Father who not only will not give him a stone
when he asks for bread, but will not give him
a stone *when he asks for a stone ?* And, sec-
ondly, need it follow that the complete subjection of our will to Christ's is also a surrender of our freedom of petition ? " *Ask*, and ye
shall receive," is no less a command than that
other, " Submit yourselves therefore to God."
Prayer is the working of a will that is free,
within a will that is sovereign. That the less
must be obedient to the greater in making its
requests, no more argues a yielding up its
freedom, than that the greater will be moved
by the less to answer those requests argues a
yielding up of its sovereignty. Not only is
there no infringement on the believer's spiritual liberty in the requirement that he ask in
holy subjection to the will of his Lord, but on
the contrary there is, as one has said, no other
such witness to that liberty "as is wrapped up
in prayer, man's *permitted* though submitted

wish and *will* and *choice*," [1] respecting all that
pertains to his destiny.

But let us not forget that the necessity of a
submitted will in prayer rests on something
deeper than itself, even on the great sacrifice
which is the groundwork of all devotion. As in
justifying faith the soul is brought into union
with Christ crucified and risen, so in intercessory faith it abides in this union. And
because our great High Priest can never forget his cross and his blood, we may not. We
may come with the utmost boldness to the
throne of grace as being in Him who "ever
liveth to make intercession for us," but we
shall come also with entire self-surrender as
being in Him "that liveth and *was dead.*"
And because we are "dead *with* Him" we
shall be careful to bring that only required
sacrifice of the Christian covenant, a crucified
will. This is vital. "Good prayers never
come weeping home," says Bishop Hall, —
which is certainly true of such prayers as
have gone to heaven "by way of weeping

---

[1] See the thoughtful essay on *Prayer considered in its
Relation to the Will of Man and in its Dependence on the
Sacrifice of Christ's Death*, by Dora Greenwell, to whom I
am indebted for I know not how many suggestions of truth.

cross." But are not many prayers put up in
which there is no tender, tearful remembrance
of that sacrificial woe which bought for us
the right to pray in Christ, — and yet prayers
pleaded in his name " who in the days of his
flesh offered up prayers and supplications with
strong crying and tears unto Him that was
able to save him from death," [1] each time saying the same words, " Not my will, but thine,
be done ? "

Because we can nowhere else deal with
God through the atonement without a submitted will, we cannot here. Saving faith is
at once a surrender of self, and an appropria-
tion of Jesus Christ. And interceding faith is
like it, — a hearty, aye, vehement yielding up
of the will to God while laying hold of his
all perfect will. Here we touch the secret of
assurance. " And this is the confidence that
we have in Him, that, if we ask anything *according to his will*, He heareth us." Outward
diversions may break the reverential intimacy
of our communion with Him ; the chill of
worldliness may cool the pulse of fervent
desire : but if the will yet moves needle-like
to the one blessed point, the holy will of Jesus,

[1] Heb. v. 7.

and rests there, the deepest condition of prevailing prayer is realized.

If the conditions of prayer in Christ are thus profound and exacting, the blessing and privilege are inexpressibly glorious. To have Christ dwelling in us, his will encircling ours with its holy constraints, and his heart within us the fountain of all blessed desires, do we count this a rich prerogative of the gospel? What shall we say then of that grace whereunto we are called, of being so in Christ that his influence with the Father passes over upon us; so that " *when we offer our prayers through his mediation it is He that prays, his love that intercedes, his blood that pleads, it is He who obtains all from his Father.*" [1]

There is something more for us now than the proxy of faith, — the standing afar off with no ray of divine approval falling upon us, and asking blessings for Jesus' sake. Lest we should think of the matter thus, our Lord declares with exquisite grace and tenderness, " I say not unto you that I will pray the Father for you, *for the Father Himself loveth you* because ye have loved me, and have believed that I came out from God.' "[2] One with Jesus

---

[1] Bishop Wilson's *Sacra Privata.*   [2] John xvi. 27.

the Mediator, and endeared to the Father's heart by all that makes Him dear, we come no longer to the throne as beggars asking alms, but as sons seeking an inheritance. We cannot be ashamed now, that wait upon the Lord, for the glorified Son has said, " *The glory which thou gavest me I have given them.*" We cannot be afraid before Him now, for the ever Beloved One has said, " *Thou hast loved them as thou hast loved me.*" We cannot doubt that we have the petitions that we ask now, for being " in Christ Jesus who of God is *made unto us righteousness,*" how can we fail to receive the promise, " The effectual fervent prayer of a righteous man availeth much " ? [1] Perhaps in the presence of such a revelation as this, our greatest need of prayer may be to ask that we may not " stagger at the promise of God through unbelief." One who has looked deeply into this theme writes : " A poor sinner permitted to approach the Father in all his troubles *as though he were Christ.* If one were internally awake he would not know how to bear himself for joy and amazement at the grant of such a privilege." [2]

---

[1] James v. 16.   [2] Krummacher.

10

And yet, in the unfoldings of Redemption from Christ crucified to Christ glorified, this blessing and mystery only deepens more and more. The "no more conscience of sins" which we get while standing before the cross, is followed by the entering into the Holy Place with Christ after the veil of his flesh has been parted. His Priesthood consummates what his blood has purchased. Into the Holiest,[1] whither the High Priest could go only once a year, and then with the deepest awe, the humblest believer may now enter "boldly" by his oneness with his Lord. And where Aaron never sat down, there he is "made to sit in heavenly places in Christ Jesus."[2] If a sense of his deep unworthiness before God often leads him to take up the cry, "Hide not thy face from thy servant," the Spirit, by convincing of the righteousness of Christ, immediately reassures him. If there is no veil between the Father and the Son in glory, how can there be any between the Father and those who are in the Son. As He is, so are they. His righteousness is their priestly vesture. He is the "Holiness unto the Lord" inscribed upon

---

[1] Heb. x. 19.   [2] Eph. ii. 6.

their frontlet. His promises are the golden
bells that vibrate about their garments as
they enter in unto God. Blessed are they
who know their privilege in Him. Thrice
blessed they who faithfully use it ; daily
"*putting on the royal apparel and standing
in the inner court of the King's house,*" [1]
assured of the outstretched sceptre and the
gracious promise, "What is thy petition ?
and it shall be granted thee ; and what is
thy request ? it shall be performed."

Thus is prayer in its deepest significance a
communion with the Father through communion with the Son.[2] Abiding in Christ we get
the spirit of supplication — the blessing of
"*a mind clothed with inward prayer.*" His
words abiding in us both fix the direction of
our petitions and bring, how often ! that answer which God has promised to suppliants
"while they are yet speaking." Abiding in
Him we have his mind as our guide in intercession, so that if our desires be left unconstrained it will bend them to seek our highest blessing, as the diviner's rod, held in the
unresisting hand, is bent to the cool sweet
water-courses that flow invisibly beneath

[1] Esther v.   [2] Note L.

the earth. In Him, we are clothed with the righteousness which constitutes in the economy of grace not only our right of petition but our claim to be heard, so that as we appear in it before the mercy-seat we may urge in triumphant humility God's oath and faithfulness, — "*Have respect unto the Covenant.*"

If now our privileges are the measure of our duties, can we set any bounds to our obligation of Christian prayer ? Where God's will is clearly revealed to us as, *e. g.* concerning our personal holiness, " This is the will of God even your sanctification," the duty can be nothing less surely than to " pray without ceasing." And the assurance of an answer can be nothing less than to know, without questioning, that what we ask we shall receive.

In other matters, among the obscure and unrevealed decrees of Providence, if our assurance must be less specific, our supplication must not be less intense in searching for God's will, that when we have found it we may take it up and urge it with all the energy of a renewed and privileged soul. It is in constant asking that we learn how and what to ask. The soul, looking steadfastly into the Father's face, comes at last to read his thoughts after Him ; to catch, as by a divine intuition, the indications of his will. "*I will guide thee with mine eye.*" [1] With his word in our hands and his spirit in our hearts and the light of the knowledge of his glory shining upon us in the face of Jesus Christ, surely we ought not to need the bit and bridle of violent providences to restrain us from willful and headstrong prayers, much less the scourge of terrible chastisement to drive us to pray at all.

So let us enter into the fullness of our blessing in Christ. Knowing that praying in the name of Christ is " praying in the Holy Ghost," the sole and blessed medium of a common life between the saint and his Saviour, and that praying in the Holy Ghost is having the Spirit to " help our infirmities," [2] since " we know not what to pray for as we ought ; " and to make intercession for us " *according to the will of God,*" how intently shall we seek to learn the highest use of that divine name by entering into the deepest communion with that divine Person. And with what earnestness and strength of desire may

---

[1] Ps. xxxii. 8, 9.   [2] Rom. viii. 26, 27.

we . constantly plead that prayer of Vinet :
" O God, unite more and more closely, not our
spirit to a name but our soul to a soul ; to
the soul of Jesus Christ thy Son and the
Son of man, our God, our Brother.   In this
intimate and living union may this soul gradually become our soul, and may we learn of
Him by virtue of living with Him, to love as
He loved, to bless as He blessed, and to pray
as He prayed."   Amen.

VIII. COMMUNION IN CHRIST

✠

He that eateth my flesh, and drinketh
my blood, dwelleth in me, and I in
him.   *John* vi. 56.

As the living Father hath sent me,
and I live by the Father: so he that
eateth me shall live by me.
                                        John vi. 57.

Abide in me, and I in you; as the
branch cannot bear fruit of itself except
it abide in the vine; no more can ye
except ye abide in me.   *John* xv. 4.

✠

VIII.

COMMUNION IN CHRIST.

O be one with the Lord Jesus is to be one with " Him *which is*, and *which was*, and *which is to come.*" [1] Of that threefold cord of our union with Him then, Faith, Hope, and Charity, no part can be spared, but in order to unbroken communion each alike must be strengthened and nourished : Faith, that links us to Him which was, and Love, that links us to Him which is, and Hope, that links us to Him which is to come.

And can we fail to note the careful emphasis which the sacraments lay upon each of these relations ? Baptism, the sacrament of union with Christ, declares by one comprehensive symbol our partnership in his sacrificial death, and in his risen life, and in his coming glory. The Supper, the sacrament of communion with Christ, exhibits the

[1] Rev. i. 4.

same truths in perpetual *résumé*. And so
at each communing we traverse the whole
extent of the redemption, and are joined
in equal fellowship to every part of his life
who, from being the *I Am* of Eternity, has
by his incarnation conjugated his existence,
if we may say so, to our human terms of *was*
and *is* and *is to come*.

Thus, in the breaking of the bread and
the pouring out of the wine, we have the suffering Christ presented to us ; and entering
by a uniting faith into fellowship with his sufferings, we can say anew, " I have been crucified with Christ." In the separation of the
elements, the blood, in which is the life, from
the body which it animates and vivifies, we
are reminded that death has taken place.
And thus we behold the dead Christ. But
an eager faith has only time to pronounce
its confession, " If we be dead with Him,"
before the commemoration has become a
feast. The emblems of suffering and death
are eaten, and being assimilated with our
bodies become life-giving ; and now we realize the risen Christ, and own ourselves " alive
with Him from the dead." But while love is
exulting in a present Lord, his words are heard

kindling hope, and leading us onward to yet
greater blessing. " Whoso eateth my flesh
and drinketh my blood hath eternal life, *and
I will raise him up at the last day."* Thus by
a single sacrament we are carried back to the
cross and sepulchre; thence onward to join
our risen Lord, and be quickened by the
mighty pulse of his glorified life, and thence
forward still to the redemption of our bodies
at his coming. The Memorial of Faith has
passed into a Feast of Love, and the Feast of
Love into a Prophecy of Hope.

It is obvious then that the ordinance of the
Supper was designed to be a perpetual tie for
binding together the two great parts of Redemption lying respectively in the first and
in the second advents of our Lord. " This
do *in remembrance of me.* For as often as
ye eat this bread and drink this cup, ye do
show forth the Lord's death *till He come."* [1]
And as partaken by the believer it realizes
and confirms his union with his Lord alike in

[1] 1 Cor. xi. 26.

The rite was not a memorial of death simply, but of death
conquered by life. The seal of the efficacy of the death of
Christ was given in the Resurrection; and the limit of the
Commemoration of his Passion was looked for in his Return. — *Westcott.*

both.   The soul being nourished by spiritual
bread, exults anew in its redemption from
the curse; and the body revived by material
bread, receives a sensible foretoken of its redemption from the grave.   And so, as having
died in Christ, and as being alive in Christ,
and as to be raised up with Christ, the com-
municant holds fellowship with every element
of his redeeming work who saith : " I am He
that liveth and was dead ; and behold I am
alive forevermore, and have the keys of death
and of the grave." [1]

But is it not possible now that through a
recoil from the Romish error of the real presence on the one hand, and through that slum-
ber respecting her blessed hope into which
the Church has fallen while the Bridegroom
has tarried, on the other, we have well-nigh
shut ourselves up to a single office of the Supper, the memorial?   This were enough indeed, were there no other.   To cherish a holy
keepsake from our ascended Lord, and to re-
count, if only by a *"lifeless mnemonic,"* as the
Protestant communion has been disparagingly
called, the scenes of his bitter agony and
death, were a most worthy service.

[1] Rev. i. 18.

But still we do not forget that memory is but a servant of love, given to minister, and not to be ministered unto ; and that in its tireless excursions to the cross and garden, it is only gathering food for communion with the present, living Christ. In that deep abiding in the vine on which our life depends, it is given us to hold fellowship both with the root that twines itself about the cross, and with the tendrils that stretch upward into glory, that we may draw through both the nutriment of present life and growth. And the evidence of a real interior union with the Lord is found in the constant flowing into us of the life that is in Him and the death which He died.

To this end was the Supper ordained.

The bread, in reminding us of Christ's wounded body, becomes a bread of sacrifice for feeding in us the spirit of self-denial. " The bread *which we break*, is it not the communion of the body of Christ," even of his dying body, through partaking of which we are made strong to " bear about in our body the dying of the Lord Jesus?" But as a symbol of present nourishment it is none the less the bread of life for feeding our spiritual hunger, " that the life also of Jesus might be made manifest in our body."

And the wine, as the memorial of that blood
by which we are redeemed, is the cup of suffering with Christ. " The cup of blessing
which we bless, is it not the communion of the
blood of Christ," even of that blood of sacrifice
which pledges us as we drink it to the martyr-
dom of daily dying with Christ? But as the
synonym of life, this blood is not less truly
also the pledge of our kindredship with Jesus
in glory, the quickener and nourisher of that
divine nature which we share with Him.

And these elements, eaten and assimilated,
become the aliment of that twofold growth
in which our sanctification consists — the
growth from life to life in the new man, and
the growth from death to death in the old man.

Is there then a real communication of Christ
to the believer through the sacrament? Even
as there is through the word when appropri-
ated by faith.

" *I am the Life,*" says Jesus. Here Christ
offers Himself to us in the symbols of human
language, in the sacrament of the inspired
letter. "*He that believeth on me hath life.*"
The eye sees or the ear hears the word, and
faith that " cometh by hearing," feeds upon
the spirit and the life which it conveys, and

Christ is received into the soul. Thus through the medium of faith that union is begotten whereby Christ dwelleth in us and we in Him.[1]

But the Supper is only the same communication made in *larger letters*, embodied in a vivid sign language which addresses all the senses as the word addresses two. It is still faith and faith alone that eats of Christ, apprehending the invisible through the visible, the spirit through the letter ; and so that union is realized and confirmed, — " He that eateth my flesh and drinketh my blood dwelleth in me and I in him." Whether then we speak of that first partaking of Christ by which the divine life begins in us, or of that repeated partaking by which it is perpetuated, it is faith, the mouth of the soul — apprehending by some human sense or senses, that receives Him ; it is the Holy Spirit — " the Agent of love, of union, and of life which consummates itself through union " — communicating through some human sign or signs, that imparts Him.

If all this were real to us, would not our communions be more fruitful of spiritual

[1] 1 John iii. 24

growth and blessing than they are ? They
would not be solely memorial. Faith would
bring from the cross that uniting sorrow
which makes us one with a present though
invisible Redeemer. Hope, like the dove sent
forth from the Ark, would fly across the unknown future, returning with its " Behold I
come quickly," that true olive token of the
" new heavens and the new earth " for which
we wait. And both Faith and Hope, deepening
our intimacy and oneness with Christ, would
be giving us that only preparation for his
coming, — " And now little children, abide in
Him ; that when He shall appear we may
have confidence and not be ashamed before
Him at his coming."

Perhaps there is no complaint more constantly made among Christians than that of
want of enjoyment and spiritual refreshment
from the communion.

Is the fault generally that they eat and
drink unworthily, or rather that having partaken in faith, they do not *inwardly digest* the
food of God ? If prayer and watchfulness and
self-denial are not active to assimilate with the
daily life that which faith has taken into the
soul, there can of course be little profit in the

bare sacrament. The fellowship of Christ's sufferings cannot be realized through a symbol received with the mouth merely, nor by a single apprehension of faith. There must be the prolonged exercise of the will in acts of self-surrender and sacrifice. Our cup can never be so bitter as our Lord's, but it must be the same in kind as that which He drank in the garden when in agony and bloody sweat He thrice yielded up *his will* to his Father. To take the cup from the table of the Lord and drink it, is but a small thing of itself; to carry out what we pledge in the act, in a continued taking of our Lord's will into our daily life, obeying joyfully its requirements and tasting with the same alacrity its sweetness and its severity, this is indeed to drink his cup.

And the bread of life is received after the same manner. "My meat," said Jesus, "is *to do the will of Him that sent me.*" Can ours be anything different? Can the mere symbol of the broken loaf nourish us, if there be in us no corresponding brokenness of the fleshly mind in obedience to the law of God? Nay, as Christ fed upon the Father by doing his will, we must in like manner feed upon the Son by doing his. "As the living Father

11

hath sent me, and I live by the Father, so he that eateth me, even he shall live by me."

So long as the emblems are looked upon as literal food, as by the Romanist, the Christian life will consist mostly in dead forms and ceremonies, with very little reference to the inward consecration of the mind and will. For "Man shall not live by bread alone," even though it be consecrated bread, "*but by every word that proceedeth out of the mouth of God.*" Obedience after faith, is the great principle of union, of love, and of growth. In this is the true community of life between the Head and the members. "If ye keep my commandments ye shall abide in my love, even as I have kept my Father's commandments and abide in his love."

So long, on the other hand, as we Protestants look upon the elements as only shadows of Christ's sacrifice, to be contemplated by faith, without also seeing in them the pledge and foreshadowing of a sacrifice in us to be realized by daily obedience and the continual offering up of ourselves to God, we shall derive hardly more spiritual benefit from the communion than the Romanist.

In other words, just as concerning the

spoken word, it is not the hearers only but
the doers that are blessed in it ; so of the
sacramental word : it must not only be contemplated and received, but it must abide in
us in order to be real food to us. All its elements, both those of sacrifice and those of life,
must be incorporated with our deepest spiritual
nature, and so ultimately tell upon our outward
activity as really and as perceptibly as the
food of a laborer does upon his daily toil.

If the Supper is thus exacting in its claims
upon our will and service, the form of its cel-
ebration is also beautifully suggestive of that
rest of faith, that peaceful abiding in the Lord
Jesus, which the believer enjoys. It is the
true Passover,[1] in which the Lamb without
blemish is offered in symbol as the food of his
people. But not like the first Passover is it
to be "*eaten in haste*," while we stand with
girded loins and staff in hand. We that believe have escaped the house of bondage.
The waters of our burial with Christ stand
between us and it to witness to our separation
from its curse. We now *sit down* with Christ,
in whom is no condemnation. He is our
peace. We eat the bitter herbs of mortification and self-denial, in fellowship with his

[1] Luke xxi. 13 ; Exodus xxii. 11.

death, and the unleavened bread of sincerity and truth in communion with his obedience; but we have something better for a troubled conscience and a trembling faith than these. " Christ our Passover is sacrificed for us." His blood sprinkled on the lintels of our hearts answers every accusation of God, and may silence also every doubt and dark misgiving of our souls. Here faith rests on that word of God, that cannot pass away. " When I see the blood, I will pass over you." And one with Christ in this communion, we realize our oneness with all saints, and call upon them to help us comprehend "what is the breadth and length and height and depth, and to know the love of Christ which passeth knowledge." *For no one household of faith can take in the whole Lamb.*[1] Each needs his neighbor in the kingdom and fellowship of Jesus Christ, to join him for the perfect communion of the redeemed. Only thus can we " grow up into Him in all things which is the Head, even Christ; from whom the whole body fitly joined together and compacted by that which every joint supplieth, according to the effectual working in the measure of every part, maketh increase of the body unto the edifying of itself in love."

[1] Exodus xii. 3, 4.

IX. SANCTIFICATION IN
CHRIST.

✠

To them that are sanctified in Christ
Jesus.   1 *Cor.* i. 2.

But of Him are ye in Christ Jesus,
who of God is made unto us . . . .
sanctification.   1 *Cor.* i. 30.

In Him is no sin.   Whosoever
abideth in Him sinneth not.
                              1 *John* iii. 5, 6.

He that abideth in me, and I in him,
the same bringeth forth much fruit.
                              John xv. 5.

✠

IX.

SANCTIFICATION IN CHRIST.

HE believer's sanctification is at once both complete and incomplete. As "*sanctified in Christ Jesus,*" and embraced in his comprehending holiness, he can no more improve this grace than he can add lustre to a sunbeam. It is a work of God, and "Whatsoever God doeth, it shall be forever : nothing can be put to it, nor anything taken from it." [1] As fulfilling in himself that sanctification which has been wrought for him in Jesus Christ, this grace is only too painfully partial and incomplete. For imperfectness is as characteristic of the creature as perfection is of the Creator.

We shall be little likely therefore to fall into error and confusion concerning this doctrine if we keep in mind the distinction between what we are as "*his workmanship*" [2]

---

[1] Eccl. iii. 14.   [2] Eph. ii. 10.

and what we are as "*workers together with Him.*" [1]   As the first we are not only "created in Christ Jesus," but "*created in righteousness and true holiness.*" [2]   Christ and his attributes never part company, and it is impossible to be made in Him without being made into all that belongs to Him. In the same transfiguration of faith by which we put on the Lord Jesus, do we put on his raiment of holiness, "exceeding white as snow, so as no fuller on earth can white it."

This may seem to some indeed like an assumption perilous to our humility. But do we honor God most, let it be asked, by limiting his grace to the degree of our worthiness and capacity? Is Christ best pleased that we take Him piecemeal, and according to the narrow measure of our deserts, when He has given Himself to us wholly and without reference to our deserts? Nay, we have no more right to find a partial sanctification in Christ than we have to find a partial justification. Both are contained in the same Legacy of love, and bequeathed to us on the same condition, simple faith. "Of Him are ye in Christ Jesus, who of God is made unto us wisdom and *righteousness* and *sanctification*

[1] 2 Cor. vi. 1.   [2] Eph. iv. 24.

and redemption," made unto us all these in their fullness, and not some of them and partially as we can receive them,—unless indeed we make a distinction, which would seem unnatural, between the manner of bestowing righteousness and sanctification, holding that the one is immediately imputed and the other only gradually imparted. Would not the truth seem to be rather, that both are imputed to faith to be wrought out by obedience and holy living?—God's justifying of us in Christ being more and more realized in the answer of a good conscience in ourselves ; and his sanctifying or setting apart of us in Jesus being more and more fulfilled in our own sanctification or separation from sin.

And it is because we can thus rest on a completed work in Christ that we have hope to go on unto completeness in ourselves, " *to apprehend that for which we are apprehended of Christ Jesus.*" Hence also the harmony between texts that have seemed strangely at variance, such as, " Ye are washed and ye are sanctified," against, " This is the will of God, even your sanctification ; " and, " For by one offering He hath perfected forever them that are sanctified,"

against, " Let us go on unto perfection." In
Christ Jesus all contradictions are reconciled ;[1]
the things that are incomplete, and the things
that are not, becoming the things that are,
and the things that are complete. As a gift
of grace, then, sanctification is conferred on
each Christian as soon as he believes. But
it is a gift yet *held on deposit*, if we may say
so, " hid with Christ in God," to be appro-
priated through daily communion and gradual
apprehension. And so, while the believer's
realized sanctification appears painfully mea-
gre, at most a thin line of light, like the cres-
cent of the new moon, he yet sees it ever
complemented by the clear outlines of that
rounded perfection which is his in the Lord
Jesus, and into which he is to be daily waxing
till he attains to " the measure of the stature
of the fullness of Christ." Is not the most
fruitful root of misconception on this subject
to be found in the idea, that while our justification stands wholly in Christ, our sanctification stands in ourselves ? As though it were
our human nature that is to be improved and
brought to ultimate perfection ! One surely
could never harbor such an error, were he

[1] " En Jésus-Christ toutes les contradictions sont accor-
dées." — PASCAL.

mindful of that form of doctrine to which he was committed in baptism. That declared the putting off and burial of the old man, and the putting on of the new man. And it cannot be that this forecast of the Christian life is so reversed that we are now called to exhume what has been buried, and to clothe ourselves again in the cast-off garments which we have solemnly declared to be beyond the hope of renovation. No! what has been crucified must be mortified, what has been buried must be kept down. So hopeless and irreparable is the doom of the flesh, that we know not that it is any better in the believer than in the unbeliever, only that its instincts are repressed, and its dominion circumscribed. "In me, that is, in my flesh, dwelleth no good thing." Whither, then, shall I turn in my deep desire to attain a sinless life, a fruitful obedience, and a holy walk? Even unto Him who, having begotten holy desires within me, is able "to give unto them their meat in due season," and who, having clothed me with salvation as with a garment, can also nourish and build me up in inward sanctity and perfectness.

Let us note then how, as every condition of our accredited sanctification rests on our

being in Christ, so every condition of our
practical sanctification rests on our abiding
or continuing in Christ.

In the first place, sanctification implies holiness. To the question, How shall I attain a
sinless life? the Word has but one answer:
" *In Him is no sin; whosoever abideth in Him
sinneth not.*" [1] As the soul that is in Him
through the union of faith, is covered with his
stainless righteousness, so that soul abiding
in Him in the unbroken fellowship of love and
obedience, is filled with his sinless life. It
sins not actively, since its activities are for the
time controlled by Him, and so the principle
of evil is inoperative and lying in abeyance.
Not that the root of sin has been eradicated.
This is entwined with every fibre of the carnal nature, " like ivy in an ancient wall," as
Flavel says, " which, however plucked and uprooted, can never be wholly gotten out of it
till the wall is taken down." But it is kept
for the time in blessed unfruitfulness, its leaf
withered by the brightness of the Saviour's
presence.

Doubtless many Christians have known
such experiences, — periods of happy exemp-

[1] 1 John iii. 5.

tion from willful transgression, because the
will has been given up to the guidance of the
Holy One ; seasons of communion with Christ
in which the fetters of fleshly bondage have
been for the while so thoroughly broken, and
its cords cast away, that the favored one has
almost questioned whether he were in the body
or out of the body. We may instance such
privileged days as those which Flavel describes,
when he was permitted to have such intimacy
with Christ, " such ravishing tastes of heavenly
joys, and such full assurance of his interest
therein, that he utterly lost sight and sense of
this world and all the concerns thereof ; " those
favored engagements with the Lord Jesus,
which Brainerd records when he felt within
himself such " lively actings of a holy temper
and heavenly disposition, such vigorous exercise of that divine love which casts out fear,"
that it was literally Christ for him to live ; that
deep entering into the divine life which Edwards enjoyed, and which he describes as " a
calm, sweet abstraction of soul from all the concerns of this world ; and sometimes a kind of
vision or fixed idea of being alone in the moun-
tains, or some solitary wilderness far from all
mankind, sweetly conversing with Christ, and

rapt and swallowed up in God." But surely
never more than after such abundant manifes-
tations of the power of the divine grace to lift
one beyond the control of the flesh and into
uninterrupted communion with Christ, does he
need to be warned to take heed, lest, thinking
that he thereby standeth in a state of sinless
perfection, he suddenly fall. There is a wide
difference between a present attainment and a
permanent attainment. And who has not
found that it is easier to rise to lofty heights
than it is to maintain one's self there ? These
grapes of Eschol, these " days of heaven,"
full of deep communion and freedom from conscious sin, remind us, by their very rarity and
infrequency, that we have not yet reached the
promised land of perfect holiness. But they
tell us where to find that land, — not back, beyond the waters of our baptism, in the Egypt
of the flesh and in the bondage of the law, —
but onward over that Jordan of death in which
we shall put off this corruptible forever ; in that
land which the Lord hath given to us for an
inheritance, where we shall abide continually
in Christ, because sundered forever from the
root of Adam. Such wild dreams as that of
perfection in the flesh would be little enter-

tained if men kept clearly in view the distinction between what we are *in Christ* and what
we are *in ourselves.* To be in Him is to be
saved at once, and forever from the condemnation of sin, but as the lives of the highest and
the lowest saints alike testify, not immediately from the presence and inworking of sin.
Christ had sin upon Him, though He had no
sin in Him. He that is in Christ has no sin
upon him, though he still has sin in him.
And just in proportion to the completeness
of his abiding in Him by communion and
obedience, will he be free from sin within him
as he is from sin upon him. But let us not be
deceived. Because the Spirit addresses us as
those that are " sanctified *in the name of the
Lord Jesus,*"[1] let us not therefore claim to
have reached a state of practical and realized
sanctification in ourselves. " We are in Him
that is true," and " In Him is no sin."
" But if we say that *we* have no sin, we de-
ceive ourselves, and *the truth is not in us.*"
Not yet have we reached that Paradise of holy
perfection for which we sigh, that sweet mil-
lennium of inward peace and righteousness
where sin can hurt and destroy no longer.

[1] I Cor. vi. II.

For that we wait till the old leaven of the flesh has been purged out and we have become a new lump.   And then when Christ who is our life shall appear, — appear " *without sin unto salvation,* — shall we appear also with Him in glory, without sin either in us or upon us forever.

Is Death then the great sanctifier? it is impatiently asked.   Is his cold hand endowed with a skill and cunning to do the work for us in a moment which the Spirit and the Word and the ordinances have failed to perfect in a lifetime?   Nay, death is but the letting go of a hand that has been constantly hindering that work, the final relinquishment of his hold on the part of that carnal man who is neither subject to the law of God himself, nor permits the believer in whom he dwells to be subject to it.[1]   This much negatively ; and then it is

[1] St. Francis de Sales writes to one who complains of sad heart sickness over the evil of an unsanctified will : " Thank God, ' this sickness is not unto death, but for the glory of God.' You are like Rebecca when two peoples struggled within her womb, *but the younger was destined to prevail. Self-love only dies with our natural death ;* it has a thousand wiles whereby to keep a hold within the soul, and we cannot drive it forth.   It is the first-born of the soul ; it is upheld by a legion of auxiliaries, emotions, actions, inclinations, passions ; it is adroit, and knows how to employ

also the rending of the veil that keeps us from full communion with the Lord. For to be with Christ where He is, whether that presence be gained by our going to Him or by his coming to us, is doubtless essential to a state of complete abiding in Him, and hence of full conformity to Him.

Who knows what depth of meaning is hidden in that, "*For we shall see Him as He is,*" in which John finds the reason and pledge of our likeness to Christ at his appearing? All our holiness is in Him and from Him, as the sunbeams are in and of the sun. But how is its lustre dimmed in passing through the medium of our fleshly life, and how are its rays broken and refracted before they fall upon the retina of our inward eye. Only in the open vision of his face and in his light who is "the Light," can our likeness to Him be rendered perfect. For only thus can we truly reflect his purity, seeing Him as He is, and having the last germs of impurity in ourselves consumed in that light which is above

endless subtleties. On the other hand, the love of God, which is later born, has its emotions, actions, inclinations, and passions. These two struggle within us, and their convulsive movements cause us infinite trouble. But the love of God must triumph." — *Spiritual Letters, XII.*

12

the brightness of the sun. It is not only
that our Lord will give us more of Himself,
but will give it "directly from Himself in
place of its coming through an 'earthen ves-
sel,' which both limits the abounding flow of
his fullness and also gives an earthy taste to
the living water." [1]

And what we have said of holiness applies
equally to another element of progressive sanctification, its very evidence and attestation indeed, Christian fruitfulness. This is from Jesus Christ only. *"He that abideth in me and
I in Him, the same bringeth forth much fruit."* [2]
In Him by faith, and hence one with Him in
that unchangeable justification which enwraps
the Head and the members together, we may
be very far from abiding in Him by that full
communion through which his life flows into
us without interruption, and abides in us
without stint. The feeble branch may be in
the trunk as truly as the fruitful one, knit into
its structure by the same compactness of
grain and fibre. But because it has little
communion with it through the vital sap, it
bears little fruit, and adorns its station with
little greenness and beauty. Christ our Vine

[1] Adelaide Newton.   [2] John xv. 5.

is not straitened in Himself, but only in us.
As impossible as it is for the fruits of holiness to grow upon the stock of human nature,
so impossible is it for anything else to grow
upon the divine. That which is born of
God cannot commit sin. It is only a question of presenting such an open channel for
the inflow of the life of Jesus, that the holy
principle shall be transmitted to us without
obstruction, and reproduce itself without re-
straint.

Is there not a painful tendency among
believers to seek fruit from without instead
of from within, and to be satisfied with such
good works as are the mere extrinsic adorn-
ments of faith instead of its direct outgrowth?
But whether we speak of fulfilling righteousness in ourselves or towards others, the same
principle obtains, that "whatsoever is not of
faith," and hence not of Christ, " is sin." For
sanctification we have not to copy another's
holiness, however excellent, but to work out
our own salvation ; to unfold to its utmost
limit that divine life which is ours in Christ.
And for service the law is the same. Love
to neighbor and self-denial for mankind are
to be no borrowed graces, lent us either by

philanthropy or the law. With the disciples,
who so significantly met our Lord's demand
for a sevenfold forgiveness of a sevenfold offense, with the prayer, " *Increase our faith,*"
we shall learn more and more that the only
way to augment the fruits of charity and long
suffering is to strike the roots of our faith more
deeply into Christ, and entwine them more intimately about that cross from which the first-
fruits of divine forgiveness were gathered, and
from which all subsequent fruit must also
spring. So directly indeed is likeness to
Christ dependent upon communion with
Christ, that John makes the two equivalent
terms. " He that saith he abideth in Him
ought himself also so to walk even as He
walked." Relationship to Him determines all
other relationships, those of conformity to God
and those of non-conformity to the world alike.
Adjust the heart therefore to Him, and the
world is sure to be in its proper place. Put
on Christ, and you are certain to put off sin.
" *If you are clothed with the sun,* the moon (all
sublunary things) will be under your feet."

If from the conditions, we turn to consider
the means of sanctification, we see how obviously these are such, because they are the

media of communion with Christ, and of par-
ticipance in his life.

"Sanctify them *through thy truth,*" the .
truth not only as it is.in Jesus, but as Jesus
is in it. For the word, it need not be said, is
the earthly repository of Christ, filled by his
informing presence, and vital with all the yet
undiscovered meanings of his hidden wisdom. Therefore is it able to be the daily
bread of the soul, and to satisfy all possible
cravings of its divine hunger. "Thy words
were found of me, and I did eat them."

"Chosen to salvation *through sanctification
of the Spirit,*" the Holy One whose office it
is to take of the things of Christ and show
them unto us. For this we must always remember, that He does not speak of Himself.
He brings "the Life" to our life, and makes
the sanctified One to be more and more our
sanctification, until we are filled with all his
fullness.

Thus slowly, and as it may seem to us quite
imperceptibly, is God bringing this divine
work to completion in us. Blessed are they
who shrink not from the sharper but not less
needed means of its accomplishment, those
trials and chastisements, those humiliations

and self-denials, which are the pangs of transformation through which Christ is to be fully
formed within us. " Though our outward
man perish, yet the inward man is renewed
day by day." " The more the marble wastes,
the more the statue grows," wrote Michael
Angelo. And impossible as it will be for
nature, let it not be impossible for grace to
cry daily, " Welcome cross, welcome trials,
welcome all things sweet or bitter, which shall
bring forth within us that perfect man, that
divine ideal, visible ever to the eye of God,
and growing more and more upon our sight
as we grow up into Him who is our Head."

X. GLORIFICATION IN CHRIST.

✠

For if we believe that Jesus died and rose again, even so them also which sleep in Jesus will God bring with Him. *1 Thess.* iv. 14.

Of Him are ye in Christ Jesus, who of God is made unto us . . . . redemption. *1 Cor.* i. 30.

For the Lord himself shall descend from heaven with a shout, with the voice of the archangel, and with the trump of God : and the dead in Christ shall rise first. *1 Thess.* iv. 16.

✠

X.

GLORIFICATION IN CHRIST.

THE redemption of the body! Not only is this the event towards which the universal longing of creation [1] is directed, but the hope as involved in the return of the Lord Jesus to which all Christian doctrine points, and to which each Christian ordinance is divinely adjusted. The first light that is reflected in the face of the new-born disciple as he comes forth from the waters of burial with Christ, is a foregleam of this hope. "For if we have been planted together in the likeness of his death, *we shall be in the likeness of his resurrection.*" The last sound that lingers on our ears as the formula of the communion is repeated, is a refrain of this blessed hope: "For as often as ye eat this bread and drink this cup, ye do show the Lord's death *till He come.*" Upon

[1] Rom. viii. 22.

every thirtieth verse of Gospel and Epistle, a
ray of this hope falls either directly or ob-
liquely ; while throughout, duties and promises and beatitudes are turned to it and po-
larized by it as the supreme reward of faith.
" Behold I come quickly, and my reward is
with me."

And yet is there not a strange tendency in
the human mind to rest content with a less
reward than God has promised ; to satisfy
our hopes with the anticipation of some shad-
owy and undefinable state of existence beyond the grave, when He has so clearly
pledged the restitution of the present mode
of being with the single element of sin and
its consequences eliminated ? A longing to
be delivered from " the body of this death,"
therefore, should not imply even a willingness
to be forever delivered from *the body.* For
as clearly as Christ is set forth as the de-
stroyer of the flesh, the corruptible and
mortal element of our nature, so clearly is
He revealed as the Saviour of the body.

It is this hope only that gives a homelike
realness to our future life ; that peoples it
with the *same* saints and the *same* Jesus whom
we have known as residents of the earth ; that

makes certain to us indeed our own identity
in that existence. And if we may not quite
say that "we can conceive of nothing entered
upon in separation from the body that is
worthy to be called life," we feel at least that
the thought of being forever bereaved of that
in which we have lived and toiled and suffered
so much, would cast a shadow upon the soul
such as only the dread of annihilation could
render darker. For such an issue would involve a twofold defeat : on the one hand, the
casting down of man's dearest hope in Christ,
that of his final reconciliation to himself ; on
the other, an apparent partial triumph of evil
over God in the eternal putting asunder of
what in the beginning He so sacredly joined
together.

But Christianity allows us not even a
dreary speculation on this point. For while
it does not silence the groaning of the soul to
be free from what is now often a burden, it
yet modulates the groan into a confession of
faith, "Not for that we would be unclothed,
but clothed upon, that mortality might be
swallowed up of life."

How intimately this hope, like all others of
the gospel, is wrapped up in the person of

Jesus Christ ; and how the sacred bonds of
union that hold us to Him for every other
blessing, bind us to Him in spite of death for
the redemption of the body also, we shall see
as we advance.

First of all, the believer's dying is in the
Lord. "*They which are fallen asleep in
Christ,*" is Paul's exquisitely tender phrase ;
words suggestive not only of painless repose,
but of a repose which is perpetually guarded
and invested by His holy presence. They
have fainted in his arms, and he holds and
sustains and embraces them until the death
trance shall be broken. "Lord, *if they sleep*
they shall do well," our hearts instinctively
respond. For the very word is a prophecy
of a better resurrection, and the state itself the peculiar purchase of our Redeemer
for his own. "He giveth *his beloved* sleep."
All die. But only those who have lived in
Him will sleep in Him, in the *cœmeterium* of
the saints, in the true Machpelah of the redeemed which He has bought for them by his
blood. Hence the deep significance of those
words descriptive of the holy dead, as "those
laid to sleep *through Jesus*," [1] connecting, as

<hr />

[1] 1 Thess. iv. 14.

they do, the repose as well as the resurrection
of the saints' bodies directly with his mediation.

And the terms change not. They cover
the entire state from the last gasp of dying
breath to the joyful awaking of the resurrection
morning. "*The dead in Christ.*" The words
form a kind of epitaph in brief for the tomb
of all the faithful, an epitaph which, if it does
not answer every question of a curious mind
concerning the departed, tells us the one thing
that we long to know, that they are safe and
shall live again. And so we may tell the story
of the Christian's burial no longer in that brief
hollow phrase which to the ancients seemed
the tenderest allusion that could be made to
the deceased, "*Non est*," he is not ; but in
words like those of Bunyan's, so fragrant of
heart's-ease and immortelle, — "The pilgrim
they laid in *a chamber whose window opened
towards the sun rising ;* the name of that
chamber was Peace, *where he slept till the
break of day.*"

And as it is the unbroken union of the departed saints with their Saviour that constitutes their felicity and our warrant for sealing
their tombs with that beatitude, "Blessed are

the dead which die in the Lord," so it is through this union that they will be raised up at the appearing of the Lord. For the resurrection is the drawing of Christ's members after Him, the prolonging and consummating of his own renewal from the dead in the persons of those who have been incorporated into his body. Thus it would seem to be an event not simply wrought upon them from without, but fashioned also from within.

Does not St. Paul's emblem of the resurrection, the quickening of the grain that has died in the earth, furnish a beautiful suggestion of this truth? The springing up of the seed is not merely the result of a life given from the sunlight and the rain, but of a life evoked by these. Even so the resurrection of the just will be life answering to life, the life of God in man, responding to the call and yielding to the attraction of Him who is "the Resurrection and the Life." "*But if the Spirit of Him that raised up Jesus from the dead dwell in you*, He that raised up Christ from the dead shall quicken your mortal bodies *by his Spirit that dwelleth in you.*" [1] This, the Spirit of life, is the vital bond that

[1] Rom. viii. 2.

holds the bodies of the saints as well as their souls in union with the Lord, the bond on whose perpetuity every hope of restitution depends. And as close as are the links of logic by which the Apostle welds the believer's resurrection to that of his Lord, it is after all that link of life, " in Christ," on which all hangs suspended. " If we believe that Jesus died and rose again, even so *them that sleep in Je-sus* will God bring *with Him*." How that other awakening, the resurrection of the un-just, is related to that of our Lord, we know not. But only they that are Christ's at his coming will hear the Bridegroom's voice, " And *the dead in Christ* shall rise first." From the dust and from the deeps they will respond, the voice from beneath saluting the voice from above, " Thou shalt call and I will answer," while in " that silence that terrifies thought " the others will remain, till God shall bring them forth to judgment.

And going beyond the event of the be-liever's resurrection to the nature of the risen body, are any of those deep anxious questions which we are wont to put concerning it an-swered except in Christ ? To many the dec-laration, " It is raised a spiritual body," seems

only to baffle the longing for knowledge that
it would answer. For while one, seizing upon
the word " spiritual," floats away immediately
into shapeless conceptions of an immaterial
existence, and another, hearing the word
" body," cries out, " Nay ! but flesh and blood
cannot inherit the kingdom of God," each
returns from his misleading pursuit of the
truth to press with redoubled eagerness
the question, " With what body do they
come ? " But in Jesus Christ the question is
answered. In his showing Himself alive after
his passion by many infallible proofs, He
shows us as in a living mirror our own future
bodies. For thus we reason.

" As He is, so are we in this world." He
is holy and righteous altogether. And because " he that is joined to the Lord is one
spirit," we know that holiness and righteousness, those divine features of the soul, once
lost, are perfectly restored to us in Him.

" When He shall appear we shall be like
Him." But He will come as He went up,
with a body of "*flesh and bones.*" And because of that divine kindredship in which
" *we are members of his body, of his flesh, and
of his bones,*" we know without question that

we shall receive back our bodies perfected in Him ; no lineament of their identity lost, no finest tracing of their life-long discipline erased, despoiled of nothing but their corruption and mortality, and whether " blind from the prison-house, or maimed from the battle, or mad from the tombs," sitting at last astonished at his feet, with perfect sight and soundness and beauty, because "fashioned like unto his glorious body."

So then, while it is clear that the flesh in its present corruptible state cannot inherit the kingdom of God, it seems equally clear that in a transformed and glorified state it will inherit that kingdom. The translation of Enoch, says Dr. Owen, "is a divine testimony that *the body itself is capable of eternal life.*" And so vital is this witness to God's Church, that like Peter's vision it has been thrice repeated before human eyes — in the Patriarchal age by Enoch, in the Prophetic age by Elijah, and in the Gospel age by Christ. And now, whatever hope concerning our future state may be obscure or uncertain, we need no longer falter in pronouncing this glad confession, " *Yet in my flesh shall I see God.*"

13

Nor is this testimony of God general merely.
In the risen Christ minute particulars are
detailed.   He ate and drank before his disciples.   He revealed Himself to their sight as a
veritable body, and to their touch as the same
body with which they had been acquainted,
by the attesting marks of his passion.   And
He showed also the mysterious spirituality of
this body in its freedom from the restraints
of matter, and its superiority to the ordinary laws of gravity and motion.   And an
eager faith easily translates these hints concerning our glorified life.   The senses that
have lighted up the world for us, though long
quenched in the grave, have leave from the
Son of man to rest in hope.   Surely they
shall be quickened for nobler offices than
they ever yet have known, and in that restitution of all things even the material body
will present its glorified members before its
Creator with the confession, Of all that thou
hast given me I have lost nothing, but Thou
hast raised it up at the last day.   With what
finer vision and keener sense the eye shall
open at that glad awakening ; to what yet un-
imagined harmonies the ear shall be attuned ;
for what alert and tireless ministries the feet

shall be prepared, who can tell ? " They that wait upon the Lord shall renew their strength ; they shall mount up with wings as eagles ; they shall run and not be weary ; and they shall walk and not faint."

To the question of the identity of the resurrection body with that in which we now dwell, do we not see the answer most delicately outlined in those two phrases of Paul's illustration of the grain, " Thou sowest *not that body that shall be*," and, " to every seed *his own body*" ? Nowhere in nature is there such an approach to literal sameness between two objects as between the seed and its product. The same vital substance has been taken up from the old kernel and curiously transmuted into the new, decay and corruption only being left behind. Every minutest peculiarity of form and taste and color has been exactly reproduced. The seed that dies is not the seed that shall be, but there is such identity between them that the two cannot possibly coexist as separate units, the second having its being only in the ceasing of the first to be.

If then our hope of physical identity in the life to come seems to be discouraged by the words, " not that body that shall be," do not the other words, " *to every seed its own body*," satisfy our deepest longings ? They seem to assure us that we shall again be " *at home in the body*," and not strangers for a single moment, looking back to a tabernacle which has been put off, and lost to us, and to which we have said an eternal farewell ; and that we shall feel ourselves possessed of the same familiar self, in spite of all the mortal and perishable that has fallen away in our transformation. And by this inalienable personality we shall be known, as well as know. The fashion of the countenance, on which all human recognition depends, will be altered indeed, but perhaps only by the unearthly glory that shall transfigure it. Stephen filled with the Holy Ghost was Stephen still, though they that " looked steadfastly on him saw *his face as it had been the face of an angel.*"

And not alone the man whose earthly countenance was moulded by the impress of long years of trial and discipline, but even the infant that only looked for a troubled moment upon life and then died, has an inviolable seal of individuality which death cannot efface.

"One look sufficed to tell me they were mine,
My babes, my blossoms, my long parted ones ;
The same in feature and in form as when
I bent above their dying pillow last,
Yet beaming with the likeness of their Lord."

Does it not give a certain dignity and worth to human being, that the tiniest body and the briefest span of earthly life is a title-deed to the resurrection ? " *As we have borne the image of the earthy*, we shall bear the image of the heavenly." And the seed of humanity that barely broke the shell of non-existence and then fell into the earth to die, because it is a seed, must be quickened after Christ the first-fruits.

With such hopes as these set before us, what is there left for us to desire concerning our future? We do not say that the dread of death is taken away. He is a real enemy to be met, and no mere disarmed and powerless foe to be despised. There may be victory in his presence, but it is the victory of hope, the triumph seen from afar, giving exultation in present defeat, and enabling him who is now overthrown to cry, " Rejoice not against me, O mine enemy ; though I fall I shall arise." But with the most heroic facing of his terrors, and with the sturdiest endurance of his pain,

as he rends from us the garment of our mortality, we are as yet *victims* and not *victors*.

But "when this mortal shall put on immortality," then will "death be swallowed up in
victory." For then we shall not only have
broken forever from his dominion, but we
shall have reconquered from him the very
spoils of which he robbed us; while, in a body
at length exalted from its sorrowful humiliations and reconciled to itself after a life-long
warfare, we lead our own captivity captive.
"In Adam all die." Not only all persons but
all holy relations have felt the death shock of
sin; and the sharp disuniting sentence that
has sundered man from God, has not less
truly sundered man from himself. But "in
Christ shall all be made alive." The bridal
of the Church to her Lord will be also the
bridal of the soul to her body, the redeemed
spirit and the redeemed flesh brought at last
to rejoice together in perfected harmony. It
is this hope that bridges the chasm of death,
and enables the heart to bound across it in
triumph.

Is the timid cry of any yet in bondage to
the fear of death, "Who am I that I should
comfort myself with such a hope? Who am

I that I should be counted worthy to attain the resurrection of the dead ? " There is but one answer : " *I* am the Resurrection and the Life."

" *Live in Christ,*" said the dying John Knox, " *live in Christ,* and you need not fear the death of the flesh."

" Help, O Lord our God, that the joyful day of thy Holy Advent may come, that we may be redeemed from this evil, envious world, the devil's kingdom, and be set free from the bitter torments that we suffer both from without and from within ; both from wicked men and from our own conscience. Destroy this old Adam, that we may be clothed with another body that is not disposed to evil and excess as this is, but which, redeemed from all infirmity, shall be made like unto thy glorious body, our Lord Jesus Christ, so that at last we may attain our full and glorious redemption." Amen.

NOTES.

NOTES.

Note A. Page 20.

"So also is *the Christ."* (1 Cor. xii. 12.) Here the whole structure of the sentence would lead us to expect the words, *"so also is the Church."* How striking this turn in the thought by which, almost as by an inspired lapse of speech, the body of believers is named *"the Christ!"* Language can go no further in expressing the perfect oneness of the Lord and his Church.

Note B. Page 20.

I find an almost identical definition of Christian experience by Mr. Jukes.[1] He says, *" Christian experience is our measure of apprehension of that which is already true for us in Jesus."* Now it is already true for us in Jesus that "by Him all that believe are justified from all things." And one believer is just as completely justified as another. But how various the degrees of apprehension of this fact! One sees it hardly at all in such a way as to find true spiritual comfort from it. Another catches glimpses of it, a little while seeing it, and a little while not seeing it. And a few perhaps apprehend it always and in its completeness. A growing experience is a going from strength to strength in this truth, till *every one of us* in the Zion of full assurance appeareth before God!

[1] *Law of the Offerings,* p. 44.

NOTE C.   Page 30.

"*I am crucified with Christ.*" (Gal. ii. 20.) It is universally conceded that the verb here, as in the parallel passages in which the believer is represented as *dead with Christ, cruci-fied with Christ*, etc., should be translated by the perfect tense, connecting the event directly with the crucifixion of our Lord. When, for the sake of bringing out this meaning, it has been necessary to vary from the common version, we have, for the sake of uniformity, taken Dean Alford's trans-lation as given in his English New Testament, marking the passages so quoted, by a * in the margin.

NOTE D.   Page 32.

1. "If Christ took our nature upon Him, as we believe, by an act of love, it was not that of one but of all. He was not one man only among many. men, but in Him all humanity was gathered up. And thus now, as at all time, mankind are, so to speak, organically united with Him. His acts are in a true sense our acts, so far as we realize the union; his death is our death, his resurrection our res-urrection." — WESTCOTT'S *Gospel of the Resurrection*, ch. ii. 39.

2. "The Son of God took on Him human nature, not a human personality. 'He took not angels, but the seed of Abraham.' Therefore He becomes the Redeemer of our several persons, because He is already the Redeemer of this our common nature, which He has made forever his own. 'As in Adam all die, even so in Christ shall all be made alive.' As human nature was present in Adam, when by his representative sin he ruined his posterity; so was human nature present in Christ our Lord, when by his vol-untary offering of his sinless self, He 'bare our sins in his own body on the tree.' Christ is thus the second head of our race. Our nature is his own. He carried it with Him

through life to death. He made it do and bear that which
was utterly beyond its native strength. His eternal Person
gave infinite merit to its acts and its sufferings. In Him it
died, rose, ascended, and was perfectly well-pleasing to the
All-Holy. Thus by no forced or artificial transaction, but in
virtue of his existing representative relation to the human
family, He gave Himself to be a ransom for all. In intention and efficacy his sufferings were endured on behalf of all
who share his human nature. In point of fact they avail to
pardon those who, through faith and the sacraments, are
livingly one with Him, so that his personal acts have become their own." — LIDDON'S *University Sermons*, pp. 225,
226.

3. " 'He took not angels, but the seed of Abraham.' It
pleased not the Word or Wisdom of God to take to itself
some one person amongst men, *for then should that one have
been advanced, which was assumed, and no more ;* but Wisdom, to the end she might save many, built her house of
that nature which is common unto all ; she made not this or
that man her habitation, but dwelt *in us.*" — HOOKER'S
Ecclesiastical Polity, Book v. ch. 52.

NOTE E.   Page 36.

"Seest thou thy Saviour, therefore, hanging upon the cross ?
All mankind hangs there with Him, as a knight or burgess
of Parliament voices his whole borough or county. What
speak I of this ? The members take the same lot with the
Head. Every believer is a limb of that Body ; how can he,
therefore, but die with Him, and in Him ? That real union,
then, which is betwixt Christ and us, makes the cross or any
passion of Christ ours ; so as the thorns pierced our heads,
the scourges blooded our backs, the nails wounded our
hands and feet, and the spear gored our sides and hearts ;
by virtue whereof we receive justification from our sins, and

true mortification of our corruptions. Every believer, therefore, is dead already for his sins, in his Saviour; he need
not fear that he shall die again. God is too just to punish
twice for one fault; to recover the sum of both the surety
and principal. All the score of our arrearages is fully
struck off, by the infinite satisfaction of our blessed Redeemer. Comfort thyself, therefore, thou penitent and
faithful soul, in the confidence of thy safety. Thou shalt
not die, but live, since thou art already crucified with thy
Saviour. He died for thee, thou diedst in Him." — BISHOP
HALL.

NOTE F.   Page 38.

If such a view of justification seems to some to tend to
demoralization, — this easy getting rid of sin, this painless
mode of suffering for guilt in the person of another; it
seems to us the only true safeguard against such demoralization. A gospel that makes us to be healed of our sins
so easily through Christ, makes us to be hurt by our sins,
more easily and more deeply through Him also than we
could be through ourselves. "Give me an atoning dying
substitute, and make me so thoroughly one with Him in
God's esteem, and by the Spirit's work, and by my own
faith, as that in taking guilt to myself, I inevitably and
immediately lay it on Him; so thoroughly one with Him,
that I cannot possibly take guilt to Him, without taking it
to myself, and then and not till then shall my soul return
unto her rest;"[1] aye, and then, and not till then, shall that
soul be kept from entering into a guilty and self-indulgent
rest. For the same gospel that bids the penitent believer
enter into rest because he has been "*crucified with Christ,*"
bids the worldly and careless believer remember that he is
"*crucifying the Son of God afresh and putting Him to an
open shame.*"

[1] Rev. HUGH MARTIN'S *Atonement*, p. 187.

Note G. Page 55.

Rom. iv. 25. " Who was delivered — παρεδούη διὰ τὰ παραπτώματα ἡμῶν — because of our sins ; and raised — ἡγέρθη διὰ τὴν δικαίωσιν ἡμῶν — because of our justification." There would seem to be no question as to the correctness of Bishop Horsley's view of this passage, namely, that " the Apostle not only speaks of the sins of men as the *cause* or *occasion* of our Lord's death, but of the justification of men as equally the *cause* or *occasion* of his resurrection. Or in other terms, " that our Lord's resurrection took place *in consequence* of men's justification, in the same manner that his death took place *in consequence* of men's sins. See *Nine Sermons on our Lord's Resurrection.*

NOTE H. Page 69.

" But ye obeyed from the heart that *form* of doctrine whereunto ye were delivered." (Rom. vi. 17.) Canon Wordsworth draws out very beautifully from this passage the truth that Christ's death and resurrection fix the *mould* or *pattern* of Christian life into which at baptism we are cast, so that if we are not rigid and obstinate, but plastic and pliant, we readily take its form and wear its impress.

NOTE I. Page 70.

Since some still question the allusion in this passage to immersion as the primitive form of baptism, we append the following testimonies of learned and judicious men of different communions : —

" For the explanation of this figurative description of the baptismal rite, it is necessary to call attention to the well-known circumstance, that in the early days of the Church, persons when baptized were first plunged below and then raised above the water." — THOLUCK.

" There can be no question that the original form of bap-

tism — the very meaning of the word, — was complete im·
mersion in the deep baptismal waters ; and that at least for
four centuries any other form was either unknown or regarded as an exceptional, almost a monstrous case." —
DEAN STANLEY, *Eastern Church*, p. 44.

" This passage cannot be understood unless it be borne in
mind that the primitive baptism was by immersion." —
CONYBEARE AND HOWSON.

" All commentators of note (except Stuart and Hodge)
expressly admit and take it for granted, that in this verse
the ancient prevailing mode of baptism by immersion and
emersion is implied, as giving additional force to the idea of
the going down of the old and the raising up of the new
man." — DR. SCHAFF, note to *Lange*, p. 202.

NOTE J. Page 135.

" Name, ὄνομα, םֵשׁ, used in application to God and to
Christ as the manifestation of God, — always denotes the en-
tity itself in the whole compass of its properties. Accord-
ingly prayer in the name of Christ, is such as is offered in
the nature, mind, and Spirit of Christ." — OLSHAUSEN.

" We pray in the *name*, that is, actually in the person of
Christ, that is, as standing in his place through his prepar-
atory and intercessory supplication, as if he came in with
us and Himself prayed what we ask. Nor is this a mere
'as if ; " rather it is the essential truth of the matter. —
STIER.

NOTE K. Page 138.

" Having previously said that prayer in the name of Christ
is ever heard by the Father, he now adds the condition
that we pray *according to his will. The one is involved in the
other,* as we have already shown. *He who prays in the name of
Christ is moved and guided by the Spirit of Christ in prayer.*

He can ask for nothing but that which is in accordance with the will of God ; can with assurance ask only that which the Spirit of Christ makes known to him in prayer as corresponding to the Father's will. When this certainty is wanting, his prayer will always be accompanied with the condition that the desire arising in his soul and taking the form of prayer, may have for its object something which the Father approves." — NE-ANDER on 1 *John v.* 14.

NOTE L. Page 147.

Prayer in Christ is "the Eternal Life which comes to us through the Son, ascending from us through the Son, the Son in us honoring the Father, the worship of Sonship as such grateful to the Father, who seeketh such worship. Freedom and confidence of acknowledgment are of the very nature of such worship ; arising necessarily from the oneness of the Spirit, causing oneness of mind and will in the worshippers and in Him who is worshipped. In such worship there is a continual living presentation of Christ to the Father, a continual drawing upon the delight of the Father in the Son, the outgoing of a confidence that, whatever is asked in Christ's name, in the light of his name, in the faith of the Father's acknowledgment of that name, will be received. The praises rendered, the desires cherished, the prayers offered, are all within the circle of the life of Christ, and ascend with the assurance of partaking in the favor which pertains to that life, which rests upon Him who is that life." — J. McLEOD CAMPBELL, D. D., *Christ the Bread of Life,* p. 130.

LaVergne, TN USA
10 January 2010
169490LV00005B/1/A